Library of
Davidson College

FLAUBERT

Kennikat Press
National University Publications
Literary Criticism Series

General Editor
John E. Becker
Fairleigh Dickinson University

Marie J. Diamond

FLAUBERT

The Problem of Aesthetic Discontinuity

National University Publications
KENNIKAT PRESS • 1975
Port Washington, N.Y. • London

Copyright © 1975 by Marie J. Diamond. All rights reserved.
No part of this publication may be reproduced, stored in a
retrieval system, or transmitted, in any form or by any means,
electronic, mechanical, photocopying, recording, or otherwise,
without the prior written permission of the publisher.

Manufactured in the United States of America

Published by
Kennikat Press Corp.
Port Washington, N.Y./London

843
F58x dia

Library of Congress Cataloging in Publication Data

Diamond, Marie J
    Flaubert, the problem of aesthetic discontinuity.

    (National university publications)
    Includes bibliographical references and index.
    1. Flaubert, Gustave, 1821-1880—Aesthetics.
I. Title.
PQ2249.D48   843'.8   75-15622
ISBN 0-8046-9075-8

76-7341

Contents

1	Introduction	3
2	*Les Mémoires d'un fou:* The Self and Fiction	18
3	*Novembre:* The Failure of the Lyrical Autobiography	47
4	*L'Éducation sentimentale* (of 1845): Jules' Aesthetic Conversion	76
5	*La Tentation de saint Antoine:* The Order of Fantasy	105
6	Conclusion	133
	Index of Names	141

FLAUBERT

1

Introduction

While he was grappling with the composition of *Madame Bovary*, Flaubert wrote a now famous letter to Louise Colet (16 January 1852) in which he describes the tension between what he calls his two literary selves, one inclining towards high-flown lyricism and the other towards earthy and comic realism: "Il y a en moi, littérairement parlant, deux bonhommes distincts: un qui est épris de gueulades, de lyrisme, de grands vols d'aigle, de toutes les sonorités de la phrase et des sommets de l'Idée; un autre qui fouille et creuse le vrai tant qu'il peut, qui aime à accuser le petit fait autant que le grand, qui voudrait vous faire sentir presque matériellement les choses qu'il reproduit; celui-là aime à rire et se plait dans les animalités de l'homme."[1] In spite of showing a good-natured indulgence to his two opposing selves, Flaubert was aware that such a division was the source of serious aesthetic problems. His remarks, in fact, preface an explanation of why the *Éducation sentimentale* (of 1845), his first attempt at writing a full-length novel, had failed: it had unsuccessfully tried to fuse his lyrical and realistic tendencies. The result was a profound lack of unity which manifested itself above all in a jerky and disrupted narrative sequence. To improve the novel, he told Louise, he would have to rewrite complete chapters and add an entirely new one. As it stood, it really contained two novels, and its two heroes, Henry and Jules, were only arbitrarily and artificially related to one another.

Introduction

Significantly, Flaubert became lucid about the nature of his conflicting selves and concomitant aesthetic distortions while composing *Madame Bovary,* his first fully realized and innovative synthesis of divergent perspectives, and looked back upon his previous work in the light of his efforts to create such a synthesis. Following his retrospective gaze, I shall trace in this study Flaubert's aesthetic itinerary in *Les Mémoires d'un fou* (1838), *Novembre* (1841), *L'Éducation sentimentale* (1845), and *La Tentation de saint Antoine,* four works in which the conflict between his opposing literary selves is central but not fully resolved. Although they fall into what might be called his early period, the *Tentation* resists such a chronological and artificial categorization. The first version was completed in 1849, but Flaubert revised it at critical points of his literary career and did not publish it in its entirety until 1874. Its inclusion here will therefore demand more justification than mere chronological earliness.

As Jean Bruneau writes in his introduction to *Les Débuts littéraires de Gustave Flaubert* (Paris, 1962), the aesthetic studies of Flaubert, of the early works in particular, have been scant in comparison with those which have tried to shed light not on the artist but on the man: "But it is a curious paradox of Flaubert criticism that while we admire that artist we study the man. A list of the books approaching Flaubert from an aesthetic point of view would be a short one."[2] Bruneau obviously intends to make good this deficiency and suggests that the subtitle of his study should read: "How Flaubert learnt to compose his novels." Nevertheless, he does not really come to grips with the aesthetic paradoxes of Flaubert's early works. For example, he correctly places the *Mémoires* and *Novembre* in the tradition of the romantic autobiography and lists their numerous sources and models; but at the same time he insists—as do the narrators of these works—that they are authentic and spontaneous expressions of the self. A more critical reading would be needed to reconcile the fundamental contradiction between an aesthetics based on imitation and one based on spontaneous authenticity. The problem is that Bruneau uncritically adopts the claims of Flaubert's fictional narrators. Thus, he bases his assertion that Flaubert leaves behind his romantic literary adolescence with the first *Éducation sentimentale* not on an

Introduction

analysis of the novel but on the assumption that Jules' profession of aesthetic faith, what he calls realism, is the credo for Flaubert's future creation of novels. But, in spite of his intention to concern himself with the aesthetics of these early works, he provides a good deal of useful information about their literary and biographical sources while remaining mystified about their inherent aesthetic paradoxes.

It is not surprising that the basically dualistic approach to literature which rigidly separates sources from aesthetics and one aesthetic trend from another should throw little light on Flaubert's efforts to resolve his dualistic tendencies. Such an approach, an offshoot of nineteenth-century literary positivism, is both typified and undermined in one of the very first studies of Flaubert's aesthetic formation, Algernon Coleman's *Flaubert's Literary Development in the Light of His "Mémoires d'un fou," "Novembre," and the "Éducation sentimentale"* (Baltimore, 1915). It is divided into two sections, the first dealing with sources, the second with aesthetics; the second section is subdivided into two further sections devoted to separate considerations of Flaubert as romantic and realist. The order of topics strongly implies a chronological development: first of all, there were sources, then aesthetics; first romanticism, then realism. In spite of the simplicity and clarity of such a presentation, Coleman is nevertheless aware of the inadequacies of dividing Flaubert's early works into periods of chronological romanticism and realism. Though noting a trend to greater realism, he finds the *Mémoires, Novembre,* and the *Éducation* all predominantly lyrical and autobiographical, and the first part of the *Éducation* more realistic than the second, in which Jules purportedly expounds the aesthetics of realism. In Coleman's view, this aesthetics is a reaffirmation of extreme romanticism. He even goes so far as to question the very terms of the argument in pointing out that the best descriptive and realistically observed passages of these early works are, at the same time, the most lyrical. Such passages are rare but seem to constitute genuine syntheses in which it is impossible to speak of a duality between inner, subjective experience and external, objective reality, or between romanticism and realism.

However, to return to Flaubert's letter to Louise Colet, his

Introduction

main aesthetic problem was to overcome a duality of vision which, as he himself says, seriously undermined total aesthetic coherence, especially in terms of temporal structure. His greatest difficulty was in linking one passage to another, in projecting a total fictional narrative. The moments of synthesis in which such a duality of vision is overcome are miniature models for the structure of a total work but, as Flaubert found, it was no easy matter to turn an isolated moment into an extended duration. It was much easier for him to alternate between a perspective of inflated "lyrical" idealism and one of contemptuous materialism. Flaubert's respect for the *petit fait vrai* tended to slip, in the aesthetic lapses he calls to Louise's attention, into a quest for the coarse material motive determining human behavior. In these cases, his "enjoyment of the animal sides of man" is less an example of generous Rabelaisian humor than of *Schadenfreude*. While his two selves remained unresolved, both his romanticism and realism were highly distorted.

Thus, in examining Flaubert's aesthetic formation it is crucial to follow his efforts at establishing an authentic focus, a point of view which might at the same time be the source of a meaningful synthesis. Unfortunately, one book which does make a detailed stylistic study of Flaubert's early work, D.-L. Demorest's *L'Oeuvre de Gustave Flaubert* (Paris, 1931), traces figurative, symbolic, and thematic structures without relating them to point of view. Their intentionality is therefore blurred or lost, and we are left with clusters of themes and images that do not clearly reveal the experimentation, unevenness, and constant fluctuations of Flaubert's voice.

Bruneau's complaints about the neglect of the early Flaubert would no longer seem to hold true since the appearance of the first three volumes of J.-P. Sartre's mammoth study of Flaubert, *L'Idiot de la famille* (Paris, 1971–73). Sartre's progressive-regressive method, which he outlined in *Questions de méthode,* means that he constantly moves forwards and backwards in time, using late biographical and aesthetic events to interpret early ones, and vice versa; but the substance of his study is Flaubert's early life and work up to *Madame Bovary*. As the title of his book suggests, he is primarily interested in understanding Flaubert in a total psychological, socioeconomic context and, ultimately, in the

Introduction

genesis and demystification of a peculiarly bourgeois manifestation of literature. Not surprisingly, he is most perceptive in those areas in which Flaubert is both psychologically and aesthetically opaque to himself. His analysis of the early short stories is enthralling. The young Flaubert wrote them in enthusiastic outbursts, with a minimum of self-consciousness or self-criticism, and they provide a rogue's gallery of pathological types which Sartre brilliantly exposes as the various guises of Flaubert's unhappy psyche. However, Sartre is less convincing when he turns to an examination of works in which Flaubert's aesthetic self-consciousness, no matter how crudely, comes to the fore.

Sartre interestingly notes that the early short stories are obsessed with various kinds of dualism, which he traces to their psychological and social roots. "Rage et impuissance" (1837) is probably his most explicit and effective example. A famous scientist decides, out of scientific curiosity, to mate an ape with a Negress. The offspring of this union is Djalioh, the main character of the story. He is literally half beast but is tormented by vague metaphysical longings for unity and transcendence which, presumably, come from his human side. Predictably, he falls in love with the wife of the scientist who arranged the conditions of his birth, and finally, in a frenzy of frustrated love and lust, rapes her. There are similar hybrid creatures in "Un Rêve d'enfer" (1837), in which a diabolical, literally soulless, being inhabits a human body, and in "Un Parfum à sentir" (1836), in which an angelically pure being is encased in an abominably ugly form. Sartre penetrates through the clichéd romanticism of the themes of diabolism and body/soul duality and exposes Flaubert's ambivalence towards a father whom he saw as both creator and destroyer and towards a mother whom he fatally coveted. But while the dualistic characters of the early short stories may throw a great deal of light on the structure of Flaubert's neuroses, the theme of dualism undergoes a metamorphosis when it applies, as it does in the letter to Louise Colet, to a tendency of his *aesthetic* constitution. However, in his early short stories, it does not have this status. Flaubert is yet a naive writer, and Sartre rightly perceives his dualism as a psychological aberration.

Flaubert really begins the work of literary self-reflection in

Introduction

Les Mémoires d'un fou (1838), the very subject matter of which is his alienation from self and language. He is a "madman" in that he does not have an original voice which would unify the meaningless and inchoate fragments of his past. The distance from an authentic self is the same as the distance from an authentic language. The *Mémoires,* therefore, marks the loss of the earlier spontaneity of the short stories and raises the problem of psychological doubleness and alienation from self into an aesthetic problem.

The *Mémoires* reflects upon the loss of unity. Once, Flaubert recalls, he knew states of "poetic" ecstasy, lyrical flights, and a sense of infinity—states such as he ascribes to his "lyrical" self in his letter to Louise. But this "poetry" was without language; it was a transparent window onto transcendence. When he entered the world of men he radically lost this unity and discovered the base material motives and opacity governing social relations. The former wordless, ecstatic imagination was superseded by an equally wordless suffering and spleen. Nor does passion offer any lasting release. He fell in love with Maria whose shawl he had saved from the incoming tide (a thinly veiled reference to his first encounter with the prototypical Elisa Schlésinger) but was soon consumed by jealousy which plunged him once again into the opacities of the "animal sides of man." But in writing the *Mémoires* he hopes to discover a language of the self which will overcome the longing for a nameless ecstasy and the ever-present threat of an immobilizing spleen.

So that his language might be based on complete honesty, he will write down everything that spontaneously occurs to him without thought of literary order or effect. However, he rapidly discovers that his spontaneity is merely a spontaneous imitation of romantic themes and clichés, and wonders whether his inability to create a language of his own reflects the absence of an emotional source. The search for such a source becomes more and more tortuous and obscure, reaching a climax in two vivid and terrifying nightmares. Sartre maintains that Flaubert lacks the psychoanalytical tools which might reveal the latent content of his dreams and overcome the alienation which pervades the *Mémoires.* While it is true that Flaubert rarely proceeds by analysis, his nightmares have the effect of shattering the clichés and false con-

Introduction

sciousness of his various romantic poses and of revealing, through concrete and unconscious imagery, the extent of his suffering and emotional distortion. The first nightmare enacts a parody of Holy Communion in which his own body is the desecrated host; in the second he cannot respond to the voice of his drowning mother. Both dramatize the absence of communion, the loss of a significant language. Although they do not automatically establish a transition to a more constitutive language of the imagination—Flaubert's purpose in writing the *Mémoires*—a psychogenetic analysis in terms of their latent content would be even less likely to accomplish such an end.

In contrast to the extreme opacity of these nightmares, Flaubert describes an extraordinary visionary experience that occurred when he returned to the scene of his encounter with Maria. So intently does he imagine her that he is convinced that she is walking beside him and engaging him in conversation. Not only is this experience of Maria more joyously intimate and intense than their original meetings, but it produces in him an exhilarating sense of self. He no longer perceives time as an annihilating eternity or as the congealment of spleen but as a movement in which being and becoming seem to coincide, in which there is perfect rapport between self and created image. However, when this vision, which is of a radically different order from the contingent events which determine his habitual state of mind, fades, he falls back into contingency with even greater desperation than he had known before. His everyday self is now contaminated with mortality, a consciousness he attempts to flee in a renewed desire for a wordless and self-annihilating ecstasy and, finally, in a return to the annihilation of time embodied in spleen. The *Mémoires* closes on this false note of splenetic self-pity.

With *Novembre*, Flaubert appears to have sacrificed his nostalgia for spontaneous unity in the name of a self-conscious art. Although it is written in the autobiographical first person, it belongs, rather, to the genre of the *roman intime,* of *Werther, Adolphe,* and *René.* Unlike the *Mémoires, Novembre* assumes from the outset a unity of perspective. The narrator looks with melancholy upon his past, but his melancholy is assimilated to the comprehensive and unified order of nature. His autumnal emotion therefore is in

Introduction

perfect harmony with the autumnal season which establishes the tonality of his autobiography. However, as he writes, this harmony breaks down and the familiar structure of the divided self reemerges. He veers between recollections of transcendent ecstasies and a horror of materiality; but both extremes, as he discovers through his experience with the prostitute Marie, lead to the same impasse and equal sterility. His narrative is marked by continually renewed efforts to establish a synthetic point of departure, to reconstitute unity. Each effort brings an increasing sense of failure, each failure a more intense effort and a proportionately greater fall. This unifying intention reaches visionary proportions in an extraordinary pantheistic episode, the lyrical high point of the work.

In an effort to reconstitute a lapsed unity, the narrator recalls an extraordinarily privileged experience which occurred when he was walking by the sea. During this experience he was absorbed into nature and overwhelmed by the pervasive sense of a divine presence. When the vision faded, however, he found the radical indifference of nature proportionately more intolerable than before. But this vision of unity remains a key memory and is destroyed only when the narrator, in extreme desperation, returns to the scene. Everything has changed. Nature no longer offers the promise of a divine fusion or even indifference. It is frankly hostile. This demystification makes any further renewal impossible, and he finally declines into death. Although Flaubert bases the unity of *Novembre* on the pathetic fallacy—by establishing correspondences between the mind and nature—the death of the narrator is a direct consequence of his loss of faith in the possibility of such an equation. His negative relation to nature undermines the initial lyrical intention and tonality of the work as a whole.

By the time he dies, the original narrator has ceased writing his autobiography, and his last days are described and commented upon by a second narrator. Superficially, the latter's intention seems to be to demystify the illusions of the former, and the transition from first- to third-person perspective seems an important step in Flaubert's aesthetic development. However, the distance of this new third-person perspective is a contrived and artificial one. In

Introduction

his sympathies for the "poetic" and contempt for the bourgeois materialistic world, the second narrator is a kindred spirit of the first. In this sense, he continues and does not unify the latter's fragmented vision.

Although far from following such a smooth development, *Novembre* goes further in the direction of a synthesis than the *Mémoires*. The movement from lyricism to mordant cynicism in the *Mémoires* is, on the whole, fragmented rather than synthetic. In *Novembre* Flaubert establishes a rudimentary dialectic between his conflicting selves. He sees that the urge towards transcendence is not totally divorced from his extreme awareness of the opacity of the physical and social world but that these apparent opposites are really mirror images of one another. Through the introduction of the prostitute Marie, who recounts her own biography, and of the second narrator, Flaubert attempts to mediate the impasse of his solipsistic dualism. Although in *Novembre* this effort fails, he continues it in his next work of fiction, the *Éducation sentimentale*, which he conceives from a third-person perspective.

Assuming the pose of the omniscient narrator, Flaubert sets out in the *Éducation* to write a novel about an idealistic young provincial, Henry, who goes to Paris to study, has an affair with his landlord's wife with whom he elopes to the New World where, his passion and economic resources spent, he wearies of his mistress, returns to Paris, and adapts to the life of a successful bourgeois. But he cannot sustain this Balzacian format of an omniscient narrator recounting the history of a social type. He becomes more interested in the secondary character, Jules, a failed playwright and failed lover who rejects society and the active life in the name of an aesthetics which, he believes, will make him a great writer.

Jules' commitment to art has all the weight of a conversion. It follows a privileged moment of self-realization when his past, which he had bitterly rejected, reemerges without distortion and unleashes in him a vital sense of being in time. As with analogous moments in the *Mémoires* and *Novembre,* it is accompanied by anguish. Very subtly, however, he moves from a state of being in time to a position outside of time, to a perspective of detachment from which he examines the events of his life and concludes

Introduction

that every effect had a traceable cause, the general laws of which can be found in nature. Wishing to preserve such a perspective, which raises him above the surge of contingent events and emotions, he opts to become an artist whose sole purpose will be to reveal the universal laws governing all the particular manifestations of life but who will in effect cease to exist as an active participant in it. Jules' aesthetics, the elaboration of which dominates the entire second half of the novel, is commonly taken as the program of Flaubert's realism. But beneath the desire to reduce complex manifestations of human consciousness to an original material source lies the greater urge towards the eclipse of self within a pantheistic unity, the persistent "romantic" temptation of all Flaubert's early works.

Ironically, Flaubert's fascination with Jules and the elaboration of an aesthetics on which future novels will be based completely undermines the actual novel he is writing. While Jules advocates omniscience and a detached observation of mores, Flaubert abandons Henry and the details of contemporary Parisian life for the exploration of an aesthetic theory. Jules' attempts to put his theory into practice, as in his comments upon the various social types of the Parisian scene, result in lifeless stereotypes, just as Flaubert reduces Henry and company to marionettes when he briefly brings them back into the novel for a final curtain. Whatever Flaubert's claims for Jules' aesthetics, their effect on the *Éducation* is negative. As he wrote to Louise Colet, the novel had not succeeded in creating a synthesis between his two opposing selves, and he would perhaps have done better had he written two novels, one objective and realistic, the other subjective and lyrical.

Such a solution, of course, would have evaded what Flaubert conceived as the fundamental aesthetic weakness of the *Éducation,* his failure to establish a meaningful temporal sequence, an *enchaînement,* between its various events. Despite Jules, he realized that the development of human consciousness could not be contained within a simple mechanistic relation between cause and effect. In fact, Jules' aesthetics, based as it is on the rejection of the temporality of subjectivity in the name of the annihilation of subjectivity, inevitably leads to the construction of reified char-

Introduction

acters. As Flaubert wrote to Louise, he had given the causes and effects of the behavior of Henry and Jules, but between cause and effect he had failed to create any synthesis. While apparently reconciling romanticism and realism, Jules' aesthetics recapitulates Flaubert's earlier inclinations, apparent in both the *Mémoires* and *Novembre,* to reject the self in the name of pure Idea or pure Matter, in some all-embracing natural unity, the temptation, in fact, of his next fictional character, saint Antoine.

Although the first version of the *Tentation de saint Antoine* chronologically follows the *Éducation sentimentale,* it interrupts the trend towards the realistic contemporary novel. A bizarre mystery play with long narrative passages, it returns to what Sartre calls the "macrocosmic" genre of *La Danse des morts* (1837) and *Smahr* (1842), in which Flaubert considers the problem of evil not in its psychological and social manifestations but as a metaphysical and cosmic reality. Flaubert was obsessed by the *Tentation,* and when his friends Maxime Du Camp and Louis Bouilhet rejected it out of hand for its extravagance and self-indulgence, he entered a period of aesthetic crisis from which *Madame Bovary* was finally to emerge. He wrote a second version of the *Tentation* after *Madame Bovary* and a final version after the *Éducation sentimentale* (of 1868). It is a key work in Flaubert's literary development.

The *Tentation* is generically different from the *Mémoires, Novembre,* and the *Éducation sentimentale,* but its subject matter— Antoine's heretical dualism—explicitly develops the basic implicit theme of the earlier works. When Antoine loses his faith, he separates matter and spirit and becomes obsessed with the quest to discover the common origin that would once again unite them. A very nineteenth-century saint, he conceives of the single origin of all things in terms of chronological, evolutionary time, and demands a rational, demonstrable, and scientific proof of its existence. In his final hallucination he witnesses the entire evolutionary process unfold before him. The origin of all life, the origin of Being, is a living cell, a fragment of organic matter from which all forms, both material and symbolic, have developed. This final epiphany is an evolutionist's dream of the connection between matter and spirit. However, in that he envisions the living cell not

Introduction

so much as the mechanistic cause of some symbolic form but as already containing in it a potential symbolic form, Antoine prefigures a contemporary structuralist view. His living cell is not so very different from Lévi-Strauss' conception of the genetic code as the original structure—and, in spite of the latter's insistence on synchrony, the idea of "original" structure is strongly diachronic —for the most advanced and complex symbolic phenomena.

Antoine's discovery that the "living cell" contains both matter and spirit means, on the aesthetic level, that there is perfect continuity between object and image and that the work of art need only imitate the continuously unfolding natural process, that the imagination is coexistential with concrete objects, and that there is no essential difference between the imagination and reality since they both derive from the same material origin. Thus, Antoine basically repeats the aesthetics of Jules in the *Éducation sentimentale.* However, in this case Flaubert clearly shows that Antoine is in error. His dualism, his reduction of the symbol to matter, are fundamental heresies from which he is saved only by grace and a wholly gratuitous leap of faith. And, in complete contrast to Antoine's ultimate discovery of the unbroken evolution of being is the aesthetic structure of the *Tentation* itself.

Of all his works, Flaubert had most trouble with the problem of creating aesthetic continuity in the *Tentation.* As Antoine abandons the world of reality for that of fantasy and hallucination, he is no longer part of a sequence of coherent "chronological" events which automatically create the "plot" of the conventional novel. The images that besiege him are chaotic, fragmented, isolated from any recognizable natural context. Nor can his development or education provide aesthetic continuity. His images dissociate themselves from him and frequently cause him to lose consciousness. Between him and them there is a void, the void of his nothingness, of his extreme object-like *bêtise.* Unable, therefore, to create aesthetic continuity through the intrigues of plot or the development of character, Flaubert experiments with a new narrative technique. The thread of continuity in the *Tentation* depends upon a third-person narrative which connects the fragments of dramatic monologue and dialogue. However, this third-person device is not an omniscient narrator. It re-creates the

Introduction

phenomena of Antoine's fantasies uniquely from his extremely subjective point of view. But at the same time it embodies the person of Antoine as he imaginatively and physically responds to those fantasies. This point of view both sees Antoine and sees what Antoine sees. It is objective in that it has distance upon Antoine and objectively names the fantasies as fantasies; it is subjective in that it limits its range to Antoine's field of vision. Antoine therefore is both object and subject. This fusion, which makes it irrelevant to refer to either a purely objective or a purely subjective point of view, is the aesthetic analogy of Antoine's discovery at the end of his dark night of the *figura* of Christ in the disk of the sun. Like the aesthetic *figura,* the figure of Christ puts an end to Antoine's speculations about the connection between idea and matter and the priority of the one over the other.

In spite of the connecting narrative thread, the sense of a lack of continuity in the *Tentation* persists precisely because of the juxtaposition of narrative and dramatic modes of discourse. This discontinuity is all the more disconcerting because both modes exist in the same *present* temporal dimension. But in maintaining distance upon Antoine, the narrative mode holds his intense efforts at reasoning out the origin of all things in an ironic light. And, in fact, Flaubert introduces a great deal of comedy, though attenuated and less coarse in the final than in the first two versions, in Antoine's encounters with his seductive interlocutors. While it is true that the structure of the *Tentation* may be aesthetically jarring, it embodies, in its disproportions, an ironic commentary on any pretension of art to absolutism. Indeed, no less a critic than Baudelaire, who had seen only parts of the *Tentation,* ultimately found it more interesting than *Madame Bovary.* In his essay *"Madame Bovary* by Gustave Flaubert" (translated here by Paul de Man), he writes: "This work, which unfortunately exists only in fragments, contains dazzling passages. I am not only referring to the prodigious feast given by Nebuchadnezzar, the marvellous apparition given by the Queen of Sheba dancing in miniature shape on the retina of an ascete, or the conspicuously overdone setting in which Apollonius of Tyana appears, escorted by his keeper, the idiotic millionaire whom he is dragging after him around the world. I mostly want to direct the reader's mind to-

Introduction

ward the *subcurrent* that runs through the entire book, the subterranean, rebellious painful level, the darker strain that serves as a guide in traversing this pandemonic carphanaum of solitude.... As I said before, I could easily have shown that in *Madame Bovary* M. Flaubert deliberately muted the high ironic and lyrical faculties which he gave full rein in the *Temptation*; the latter work, truly the secret chamber of his mind, evidently remains the most interesting of the two for poets and philosophers."

By any conventional aesthetic yardstick, however, the *Tentation,* like the *Mémoires, Novembre,* and the first *Éducation,* is a failure. Of these, only the *Tentation* was published during Flaubert's lifetime, and in spite of Flaubert's own affection for the work and Baudelaire's praise, the more common reactions to it were outright rejection, as in the case of Bouilhet and Du Camp when Flaubert read to them the first version, or tepid praise. And in spite of the interest on the part of such critics as Valéry and Brombert, its aesthetic reputation has always been highly ambiguous. As for the *Mémoires, Novembre,* and the *Éducation,* Flaubert himself did not consider them worthy of publication. Although he read parts of these works to friends and was especially indulgent towards *Novembre,* he had no illusions about their aesthetic perfection.

The advantage of such failures for the critic, and this is especially true of the critic of Flaubert, is that they both explicitly and implicitly reveal the stages of the aesthetic itinerary. Indeed, they provide a context in which the major novels of Flaubert emerge in a slightly new light. In spite of brilliantly sophisticated studies of *Madame Bovary* and the *Éducation sentimentale* in particular, the total itinerary of Flaubert's aesthetic development remains to be traced. The movement from the *Mémoires* through *Novembre* to the *Éducation* is basically dialectical, each work incorporating and commenting upon the previous one. They may be vitiated by moments of bad faith and consequent aesthetic distortions, but such errors originate a corrective synthesis. In fact, this process does not end with the creation of *Madame Bovary.* Flaubert's entire literary career consists of efforts to supersede previous aes-

Introduction

thetic limits. In this sense, one can understand why all his works seemed to him, on the deepest level, failures. Stages in an endless process of revision, as soon as they were finished they became, by that very token, unfinished.

The *Tentation* is particularly fascinating because, bearing the marks of its various phases of composition, it comments upon Flaubert's entire aesthetic development. It is a work of transition, originating in an exotic romantic genre, which was already dated when Flaubert published the work, but pointing to an essentially modern breakdown of genre and reflection on the very nature of imaginative language.

NOTES

1. See Flaubert, *Correspondance* (9 vols.), Louis Conard, 1926-33.
2. Throughout this study all secondary sources will be quoted in translation. Flaubert alone will be quoted in French.

2
Les Mémoires d'un fou:
The Self and Fiction

> *Or, ma vie ce ne sont pas des faits; ma vie c'est ma pensée.*

Flaubert's earliest writing testifies to his interest in romanticism, a romanticism which, somewhat incongruously, had strayed into the curriculum of the *collège* at Rouen. Many of his early works, such as "Matteo Falcone" (1835), based on the story by Prosper Mérimée, and "Le Moine des Chartreux" (1835), inspired by Dumas' *La Tour de Nesle*, were assigned exercises. His history teacher Adolphe Chéruel, an ex-student of Michelet, encouraged his interest in history, especially the Middle Ages and Renaissance as popularized in fiction by Chateaubriand, Dumas, and Hugo. But what Flaubert sought above all in romanticism was the aberrant and the grotesque, and he extended his literary repertoire with elaborations of the psychological and fantastic tale in the style of Goethe, Quinet, and the early Balzac. Typical of the titles of his early sketches and short stories are "Bibliomanie" (1836), "Rage et impuissance" (1837), "Un Rêve d'enfer" (1837). Typical of his fictional heroes are the mad king Charles VI of "Deux Mains sur une couronne" (1836), Marguerite, the acrobat ostracized because of her ugliness, of "Un Parfum à sentir" (1836), Garcia, the fratricide of "La Peste à Florence" (1836), Djalioh, half man, half beast, of "Quidquid volueris" (1837), Mazza, the precursor of Madame Bovary, who sacrifices everything in the name of a mad passion, of "Passion et vertu" (1837).[1]

Les Mémoires d'un fou: The Self and Fiction

Although Flaubert passionately identified with his monstrous romantic heroes, he was nonetheless aware that he was writing in a borrowed voice. In "Un Rêve d'enfer," for example, the excesses of his macabre description of his Faustian hero the Duc d'Almaroës reach the proportions of parody: "Un enfant d'enfer, la pensée d'un démon, l'oeuvre d'un alchimiste damné, . . . dont les lèvres gercées semblaient ne se dilater qu'au toucher frais du sang, . . . dont les dents blanches exhalaient une odeur de chair humaine."[2] And in "Quidquid volueris" he is explicitly ironical towards his romantic vocabulary: "Encore la lune! mais elle doit nécessairement jouer un grand rôle, c'est la *sine qua non* de toute oeuvre lugubre, comme le claquement des dents et les cheveux hérissés; mais enfin, ce jour-là, il y avait une lune."[3] In other words, no matter how much Flaubert indulges himself in the excesses of his characters and situations, he is aware that his expression is false. His alienation resides in his distance from his mode of expression. His self does not coincide with his fiction.

Flaubert's effort to reveal directly "l'expression de son coeur et de son cerveau" begins with *Agonies* (1838). *Agonies* is a confessional work, but Flaubert himself acknowledges that it is merely a litany of skeptical thoughts, a grotesque mask, the portrait of a madman. The search for a spontaneous, authentic self discloses only the monstrous alienated hero of his earlier fictions. His identity has been usurped by the romantic persona, his authentic voice by the voice of an actor playing a romantic part. In fact, *Agonies* can hardly be called a confession at all, so little does it reveal of the particularities of Flaubert's own experience.

The *Mémoires d'un fou*, however, written in the fall of 1838, is a new point of departure, an autobiography in which Flaubert tries to particularize his experience.[4] Although it reveals the influence of his favorite confessions, Montaigne's *Essais*, Rousseau's *Confessions*,[5] and Musset's *Confession d'un enfant du siècle*, it is an ambiguous autobiography, this autobiography of a madman, in that it acknowledges that its narrator has lost a coherent relation to his past and that his present perspective is, by definition, unreliable. Indeed, in his dedication to Alfred Le Poittevin, Flaubert asks, albeit rhetorically, if the narrator is himself or another. The point of departure of this autobiographical inquiry is the ab-

Les Mémoires d'un fou: The Self and Fiction

sence of any self-definition.

He had first intended, as he informs Le Poittevin, to write a *roman intime* but "l'impression personnelle perça à travers la fable, l'âme remua la plume et l'écrasa" (p. 230). He therefore has no plan of composition, no literary form to guide him: "Je ne sais plus que vous ce que vous allez lire, car ce n'est point un roman ni un drame avec un plan fixe, ou une seule idée préméditée, avec des jalons pour faire serpenter la pensée dans des allées tirées au cordeau" (p. 230). Thus, the force of his personal feeling has forced him to abandon premeditation and fabulation. This spontaneity, however, is no guarantee of authenticity, and Flaubert admits that his expression sometimes appears exaggerated and concocted: "Le mot parait souvent surpasser le sentiment qu'il exprime." Similarly, he may write down everything as it comes into his head, but he cannot escape the artificial rhetorical device or the clichéd romantic metaphor: "Seulement je vais mettre sur le papier tout ce qui me viendra à la tête, mes idées avec mes souvenirs, mes impressions, mes rêves, mes caprices, tout ce qui passe dans la pensée et dans l'âme; du rire et des pleurs, du blanc et du noir, des sanglots partis d'abord du coeur et étalés comme de la pâte dans des périodes sonores, et des larmes délayées dans des métaphores romantiques" (p. 230). Disdaining fiction in the name of a personal truth, "literary" language constantly deforms his feeling, a paradox in which the madman of the *Mémoires* finds himself trapped.

Although he writes at random all that enters his mind and soul, Flaubert follows the rudiments of a chronological sequence based on a distinction he establishes between three stages in his consciousness: "Enfant, j'aimais ce qui se voit; adolescent, ce qui se sent; homme, je n'aime plus rien." This sequence is itself an oversimplification since his present state of mind constantly clouds and interrupts his account of earlier states. He fluctuates from the overwhelming sorrow which, as he writes in his dedication, originated the work, to the skepticism of his philosophical digressions, to the emotional deadness of spleen, to the mocking detachment of the old man he at times pretends to be. The apparently chronological present, the perspective from which he writes, functions rather as the most extreme point of alienation from the

Les Mémoires d'un fou: The Self and Fiction

more integrated states of sensation and feeling. That he situates the more integrated consciousness at the greatest distance in time, in childhood, is the expression of the degree of his present alienation. To use a term from Jacques Lacan, both his self and his language are "decentered." He expresses this decentering in terms of a genetic structure in which he places the center in a remote, chronological past.

Although, as a child, he was aware of the threatening crowd, "mer d'hommes orageuse, plus colère encore que la tempête et plus sotte que sa furie" (p. 231), Flaubert recalls his childhood as a time of plenitude and harmony when he was "gai et riant, aimant la vie et ma mère," the "pauvre mère" he has lost. He recalls the sensuous, unmediated experience of nature, the source of a physical energy so intense that it resulted in an ecstatic spiritual exhilaration: "J'aimais aussi—et c'est un de mes plus tendres et délicieux souvenirs,—à regarder la mer, les vagues mousser l'une sur l'autre, la lame se briser en écume, s'étendre sur la plage et crier en se retirant sur les cailloux et les coquilles. Je courais sur les rochers, je prenais le sable de l'océan que je laissais s'écouler au vent entre mes doigts, je mouillais des varechs et j'aspirais à pleine poitrine cet air salé et frais de l'océan, qui vous pénètre l'âme de tant d'énergie, de poétiques et larges pensées, je regardais l'immensité, l'espace, l'infini, et mon âme s'abîmait devant cet horizon sans bornes" (p. 231). Between the child and nature in this evocation of the past there is openness and reciprocity. His movements repeat the rhythms of nature, as when he gathers up sand and lets it fall back through his fingers, imitating the ebb and flow of the tide. The noise of the waves, the cry of the shells, the wind, and the salt air enter him and turn his own voice and breath into "poetic and expansive thoughts." These thoughts are without words; they describe a generalized state of mind, an ecstatic intimation of infinity. This ecstasy, however, leads the child to the edge of an abyss: "... mon âme s'abîmait dans cet horizon sans bornes." The absence of any boundary between the child and nature turns from intimacy to anxiety, from eternity to nothingness. The temporal plenum turns into a temporal disaster, the annihilation of consciousness.

The ambivalence of the child's reverie on nature emerges in an-

Les Mémoires d'un fou: The Self and Fiction

other and more familiar memory. Flaubert recalls his pleasure in riding in a horse-drawn carriage along the country roads, the intimacy of the steam rising from the necks of the horses and their rhythmical, monotonous trotting which transported him both along and out of himself. When the horses came to a halt, everything grew silent and the carriage "se raffermissait sur les ressorts." The carriage stiffened into immobility, the wind menacingly whistled against the windowpanes, and the harmonious rhythm experienced by the child and horses ended with the emptiness of ". . . et c'était tout." The child's very being seemed to depend on rhythmical sensation. When such sensation was absent, he was threatened by nonexistence.

After the description of these reveries Flaubert's tone changes. The nonexistence they intimate throws him back to his present melancholic mood and to a reflection upon the deficiencies of language. He recalls the joyous moments he spent on the edge of creation where "la poésie se berçait et déployait ses ailes dans une atmosphère d'amour et d'extase." But then he had to descend into words, "cette terre de glace, où tout feu meurt, où toute énergie faiblit." He cannot find the steps which will prevent the descent into language from being an annihilation: "Par quels échelons descendre de l'infini au positif? par quelle gradation la poésie s'abaisse-t-elle sans se briser? " (p. 231). Again, as in his reverie on nature, Flaubert equates poetry with the ecstatic apprehension of the infinite. Writing means a fall. In imagery that uncannily anticipates Mallarmé's swan trapped in a frozen lake, Flaubert describes poetry as a bird which breaks on the frozen earth of language.

With the failure of language to embody his poetic ecstasies, Flaubert generalizes his sense of nonexistence into a philosophical truth. He borrows the language of Pascal to describe the ignorance and limitations of man, tossed like a grain of sand into the infinite and teetering on the edge of the abyss. It is this sense of man's nothingness, he claims, that has made him old before his time. Still, he does not find peace in his universal skepticism: "On y roule dans un vide incommensurable. Ce vide-là est immense et fait dresser les cheveux d'horreur quand on s'approche du bord" (p. 231).

Les Mémoires d'un fou: The Self and Fiction

The language of this digression is disturbing. Not only are many of its ideas and images borrowed from Pascal, but Flaubert describes himself in the overwrought romantic cliché that he mocks in "Quidquid volueris": his heart is wrinkled with premature old age; his hair stands on end at the contemplation of the abyss, and like one of his own diabolical romantic heroes, he bitterly laughs at man's illusions. This digression names a movement away from the integrated self and a return to a false, second-hand voice. Flaubert's terror of the abyss, in this passage, is not so much the fear of philosophical nihilism as the terror of the loss of the self: "J'eus cependant une horreur naturelle avant d'embrasser cette foi au néant; au bord du gouffre, je fermai les yeux;—j'y tombai" (p. 231). In his reflections on poetry that immediately precede the digression, Flaubert describes the void as that which threatens to devour him when he cannot find the words to express and sustain the ecstatic poetic flight of ideal thought. He assumes that he cannot find the words because of the natural deficiencies of language, "un écho lointain et affaibli de la pensée," which, by definition, can never coincide with his most intimate and nameless intuitions. Therefore, no authentic language is possible, and the self must lapse into nonbeing. The inauthentic language of the philosophical digression is a logical expression of the dubiously self-justifying assumption. It leads to an empty impasse which Flaubert leaves by returning to the second stage in his autobiography, memories of school.

At school he discovered society, and it is to this discovery that he traces the origin of his madness: "Dès lors j'étais un fou" (p. 232). A pale imitation of Rousseau's natural man confronted with the egoism and injustices of the state, Flaubert identified with his romantic heroes Byron, Werther, Hamlet, and elevated his miserable isolation into a sense of scornful superiority. He retreated into daydreams, that is, "rêves d'avenir," which replaced the banal routine of school lessons. Unlike the plenitude of the earlier reverie, they projected a future fulfillment mediated by a desire for evasion, success in society, and revenge. He drew on the exotic panoply of romantic literature as he imagined himself at twenty, celebrated, travelling in a sumptuous Orient, and loved by "quelque femme à la peau brune, au regard ardent,

Les Mémoires d'un fou: The Self and Fiction

qui m'entourait de ces deux bras et me parlait la langue des houris" (p. 232). He transported himself in time, revelled in the deaths of civilizations, and praised the gigantic destructiveness of Nero in a debauched and decadent Rome. He was aware, however, that his society considered him a monstrous anomaly, good only "à faire un bouffon, un montreur d'animaux ou un faiseur de livres" (p. 233). To his schoolfellows he looked like an idiot as, during the exotic voyages of his imagination, he sat for hours on end apparently staring at his desk or at a spider spinning a web on the schoolmaster's chair. This "catatonia" was the dangerous correlative of his "rêves d'avenir." The image of the spinning spider that filled his outer eye expressed both his negation of his social and physical context and the reduction of time into mechanical and compulsive repetitions. An insect in the eyes of the others, he turned into a murderous Nero in the imagination. This alienation reached its extreme expression in two nightmares, "d'effroyables visions à rendre fou de terreur" (p. 233).

In the first dream, he was lying in his bed at home ("dans la maison de mon père"). There was a black pall over the furniture. It was a winter night and the snow cast a white light into the room. Suddenly the snow melted and the grass and trees turned a burnt russet color as though a fire were lighting up the windows. He heard the sound of footsteps on the stairs, and a fetid smell filled the room. The door opened, and seven or eight men entered. They were big, or small, with rough black beards and each with a steel blade between his teeth. They made a circle around his bed, and the chattering of their teeth was horrible. They drew back the curtains, and their fingers left bloody imprints. They stared at him with lidless eyes. He stared back, petrified and wanting to scream. It seemed that the house was being levered from its foundations. The intruders looked at him for a long time and then separated. One side of their faces was raw and streaming with blood. They lifted up his nightclothes, staining them with blood. They began to eat, and the bread they broke dripped blood; they began to laugh, a death rattle. When they disappeared, everything they had touched was bloody. He had a bitter taste in his mouth as though he had eaten flesh; he heard a harsh, prolonged cry; the doors and windows opened and screeched in the wind, making

Les Mémoires d'un fou: The Self and Fiction

a bizarre song that pierced his heart like a knife. In the second dream, he was walking in the countryside ("verte et émaillée de fleurs") with his mother, by the side of a river. His mother fell into the water, which foamed, formed widening concentric circles that all of a sudden disappeared, and then continued its course. Suddenly he heard the voice of his mother calling for help. He lay down on his stomach but could see nothing. The cries continued. An invisible force fixed him to the ground as he heard: " I am drowning! I am drowning! Help!" The water continued its limpid course, while the voice he heard from the depths of the river filled him with rage and despair.

Dreams in literature pose special problems of interpretation. One can either interpret them entirely within the context of the literary work, as Freud does, for example, in his interpretation of delusion and dream in Wilhelm Jensen's *Gradiva* (1906), or one can use them as the bridge between psychology and literature in order to uncover the process of creation. This, according to Freud in the introduction to the second edition of his study of *Gradiva* (1911), should be the aim of the psychoanalytical approach to literary works: "It no longer seeks in these works a confirmation of its discoveries in unpoetic, neurotic individuals, but also demands to know out of what store of impressions and memories a creative writer has fashioned his work and in what way, through what process, this material was introduced into the work of literature."[6] The *Mémoires,* simultaneously a quest for an authentic self and an original literary voice, demands a fusion of both these approaches.

Flaubert himself attributes the cause of his dreams to a nervous irritation occasioned by the uncongeniality of school, and makes no further analysis of them. They originate in the cold and lugubrious school dormitory where he lay listening to the wind and the footsteps of the night watchman on his rounds. Obviously, the details of this setting influence the details of the first dream —the bed, the footsteps, the wind against the window—but do not explain the shift from school to family context: he dreams that he is in his *father's* house. This family reference is repeated in the second dream in the drowning of his mother.

In effect, the dreams conjure up a description of childhood in

25

Les Mémoires d'un fou: The Self and Fiction

complete contrast to Flaubert's previous description of his childhood reverie. They elaborate upon two earlier peripheral details: the angry sea of men and the intimated loss of his "pauvre mère." The first is central to the first dream, the second to the second. The dreams therefore combine both the anxiety experienced at school and an earlier anxiety associated with the family, only hinted at in the beginning of the text. However, the result of this combination is a new expression particular to itself.

Both dreams construct a narrative sequence. They are compact short stories which might have come directly from Flaubert's repertoire of romantic horror tales. The bearded men with knives between their teeth, the diabolical force of nature dragging away the mother, are *topoi* of the grotesque. The important difference between these dreams and Flaubert's early tales is that he introduces himself as the main protagonist. Moreover, the other protagonist of the second dream is his mother, whom he presents without disguise, and the protagonists of the first dream, the group of identical bearded men, are hardly disguised representations of the father. By not particularizing them as the father, by representing them as a multiplicity, he makes the association between the father and society, the angry oppressive force he encounters at school. The action of these dreams is the drama of the destruction and loss of his self.

The imagery of the first dream—the deathly pallor of the snow, the glow of fire around the house, the shaking foundations, the murderous intruders, the breaking of the bread, and the blood—reflects the threatened foundations of the dreamer's being. At the center of the dream is the desacralization of the sacrament, a kind of sacrament in reverse, which celebrates the destruction of communion. The dreamer is a communicant whose voice is stolen from him. He has no response but a stifled scream to the diabolical priests. This destruction of communion and communication is repeated in the second dream, in which the mother's voice is the haunting sign for a lost unity which has been absorbed into a deathly, purely material nature, and to which he can respond only by violent rage and despair.

Only if one understands the transparent Oedipal references of the dream as the expression of the loss of a language of communi-

Les Mémoires d'un fou: The Self and Fiction

cation, can one explain them in terms of the Oedipus complex. The broken bread, the symbol for castration, connotes, in this context, the reduction of the symbol to matter. It is an appropriate figure for the primary symbolism of the dream in which the self literally sleeps and which is spoken by the language of its alienation. One might call it an anecdotal, pseudosymbolic language, the counterpart of the constitutive, symbolic language of fiction.

Although it "distorts" reality, this language is incapable of the bad faith common to the "conscious" distortions of reality. It therefore exposes the hollowness of the various self-justifying rationalizations of the narrator, the truth of his alienation from childhood, society, and nature, and the falsity of the "romantic" imagination with which he tries to veil it. In the synthesis of the dreams, the effort to discover the thread of being in the chronological past collapses. They totalize alienation. It is not surprising, therefore, that they should preface the collapse of the first part of the *Mémoires*.

Flaubert is dimly aware that his dreams in some way summarize his experience, for he begins the following paragraph with the phrase: "Voilà donc comme j'étais." However, he has not consciously understood the significance of the dreams, for he lapses into a self-justification in complete contrast with the desperate anxiety they reveal. Turning away from his nightmares, he recalls himself as "rêveur, insouciant, avec l'humeur indépendante et railleuse, me bâtissant une destinée et rêvant à toute la poésie d'une existence pleine d'amour, vivant aussi sur mes souvenirs autant qu'à seize ans on peut avoir" (p. 233). He may have dreamt of an ideal future and lived off his sparse happy memories, but the scathing judgment of his fellows who condemned him to the destiny of "un bouffon, un montreur d'animaux ou un faiseur de livres" haunts him. And he can only rid himself of this judgment by explaining his frustrations as those of the noble soul, and by attempting to detach himself from them through analysis: "Ce serait une curieuse étude que ce profond dégoût des âmes nobles et élevées, manifeste de suite par le contact et le froissement des hommes" (p. 233). Nevertheless his claims to rationality, health and innate superiority are immediately followed by prophecies of imminent death and apocalypse.

Les Mémoires d'un fou: The Self and Fiction

The earth, he predicts, will be ravaged by fire, races will be extinguished "au berceau," after palaces have collapsed under the weight of their riches, man will finally awake from his orgiastic blood lust. After the holocaust, a few men, wandering over the earth, will call out but recoil in terror from one another. Finally, nature will cover up the relics of civilization. The rivers will flow through "les prairies émaillées," and nature will be free of the curse of man, for "cette race sera éteinte car elle était maudite dès son enfance" (p. 235). Man has cannibalized God: "L'humanité s'est prise à tourner des machines, et voyant l'or qui en ruisselait, elle s'est écriée: 'C'est Dieu! ' Et ce Dieu-là, elle le mange"(p.235). The world swarms like an insect over a corpse in this glittering masquerade. Gold and wine flow and "la débauche froide lève sa robe et remue" (p. 235).

These predictions of apocalypse and the description of contemporary society uncannily pick up the imagery of the dreams. The images of destruction by fire, of collapsing edifices, of a bloody orgy, of the loss of communication, of the victory of a cold and impassive nature, are now applied to the collapse of civilization. This transformation of a personal into a social imagery might be called a veiling of the personal, but it is a veil woven by society "dont chacun prend sa part et se cache le plus qu'il peut" (p. 235). The figure of the father in the dream, an allegorization of the oppressive forces of society, is analogous to the allegorization of debauchery as a writhing woman selling herself for gold. In each case, the human being is reified into a type (a device also used but in very different ways by both Balzac and Baudelaire, in which the becoming, the ambivalence of language, is frozen). It is not surprising that this process should lead to the spleen which dominates the close of the first part of the *Mémoires*.

Flaubert lapses into a state of spleen in which the content of his consciousness is reduced to the dead, material objects which randomly come within his range of vision. However, his concentration on these objects—"un rien, la moindre circonstance, un jour pluvieux, un grand soleil, une fleur, un vieux meuble"—gives rise to memories. Once again he recalls childhood: "Jeux d'enfant sur l'herbe au milieu des marguerites dans les prés, derrière la haie fleurie, le long de la vigne aux grappes dorées, sur la mousse

Les Mémoires d'un fou: The Self and Fiction

brune et verte, sous les larges feuilles, les frais ombrages; souvenirs calmes et riants comme un souvenir du premier âge, vous passez près de moi comme des roses flétries" (p. 235). The child is no longer engaged in a cosmic interplay; he is protected by nature, alternately *in the midst of* daisies, *behind* the hedgerows, *along* the vines, *on* the dark moss, *under* the vines, *in* the shadow. These memories incorporate the intimacy and reflectiveness of the act of remembering. Flaubert calls them "roses flétries" and "reflets de soleil couchant"; they reflect the loss of a plenitude of experience. The experience of remembering saturates the content of memory. Thus, he recalls a contemplative moment in which he watches the movement of water and the brilliant light of a setting sun: "Quelque promenade bien rêveuse sous une large allée couverte d'ombre, à regarder l'eau couler sur les cailloux, ou une contemplation d'un beau soleil resplendissant avec ses gerbes de feu et ses auréoles rouges" (p. 235). However, in spite of such moments of fleeting introspection, he cannot escape his spleen. The randomness of their source determines whether his memories will be merely melancholic or "mornes et froides comme des journées pluvieuses." In comparing his memories to faded roses, reflections of the setting sun, and rainy days, he highlights their contingency and ephemerality. They are only isolated images which constitute no meaningful temporal sequence. They therefore accentuate his spleen, the reification of time which he likens to death: "Oui, je meurs, car est-ce vivre de voir son passé comme l'eau écoulée dans la mer, le présent comme une cage, l'avenir comme un linceul?" (p. 235).

Flaubert closes the first part of the *Mémoires* with a memory which, he claims, has been branded on him and which he will never forget. It is the memory of a chateau he used to visit as a child when it was still the property of an old woman "of the eighteenth century," and a relic of "le souvenir pastoral." It contained dusty portraits, roses, carnations; shepherds and shepherdesses and their flocks decorated the wainscoting; but it was in a state of decay. Stones would fall, from time to time, from the crenellations and roll into the moat, and the pastoral goat in the park grounds wandered beneath somber bowers and among broken stone benches covered with brambles and moss. It was both sad

Les Mémoires d'un fou: The Self and Fiction

and terrifying, especially when the wind howled in the cavernous chimneys and the owls hooted in the loft. He informs us that the old lady is now dead, her snuffbox is in the notary's pocket. her castle is a factory, and her lovely eighteenth-century slipper decorated with a black rose has been thrown into the river.

The description of the chateau recapitulates the description of memory as melancholic, faded, the reflection of a lost unity which is represented in the evocation of the pastoral. It has succumbed, however, to an unalloyed materiality. The movement from unity to memory to materiality coincides, in the description of the chateau, with a historical movement from the eighteenth to the nineteenth century, in which the nineteenth century, as elsewhere in the *Mémoires*, stands for the destruction of civilization and the reduction of communication to money exchanges. At the same time the old chatelaine is a substitution for the lost mother. The original communion with the mother is transformed into an aesthetic attachment to the beautiful objects evocative of the woman, especially the slipper decorated with an *artificial* rose. Parallel to the nostalgia of memory, this aesthetic transfiguration is superseded by materialism. Just as the mother drowned in the narrator's nightmare, the object symbolizing the lost communion has been cast into the river, leaving a void, that is, spleen.

Thus, although Flaubert in the description of the chateau synthesizes in a single narrative sequence the movement of the *Mémoires* from recollection of unity to the loss of unity, it is a sign for the powerlessness of memory to constitute a self. It is not surprising therefore, that at this juncture Flaubert should abandon his manuscript. When he resumes it after three weeks' silence, it is with the enigmatic statement, "Ici commencent vraiment les *Mémoires*."

In his study of the *Mémoires* in *L'Idiot de la famille*, J.-P. Sartre interprets the breakdown of the *Mémoires* as Flaubert's failure to either universalize his singularity in a fictional *roman intime* or to uncover the psychological roots of his alienation, of the anomalous self, the "monstre incomparable." What Flaubert lacks, according to Sartre, is "a genetic psychology which would retrace the dialectical progression of a psychic ensemble and describe its *articulations*."[7] What at times surface through the various evasions are

Les Mémoires d'un fou: The Self and Fiction

Flaubert's horror of his monstrosity and the equal horror of the bourgeois future that his father has mapped out for him. Flaubert disguises this "truth" through histrionic poses and the assumption that his madness is the privileged insight into the madness of the age. Moreover, Sartre goes on to interpret the description of the chateau as the prefiguration of the second part of the *Mémoires,* which, in his opinion, reveals even less insight into psychological reality than the first since it substitutes anecdotes for analysis. In other words, he understands the second part as the development of a fictional intention already apparent in the description of the chateau. The real aim of the *Mémoires* thus becomes "a spiritual exercise which aims to 'irrealize' [Sartre's neologism] the content of memory. Thus the *I* of the narrator is in turn irrealized to the extent that he becomes the imaginary Creator of his life."[8] However, as we have seen, the description of the chateau is not so much a fictional anecdote as the sign for the inadequacies of the chronological autobiography to constitute a new and original self. This is not so much Flaubert's failure to see himself as a bourgeois full of bad faith as a recognition that his various kinds of "thought"—the childhood reveries, the abstract digressions, the romantic daydreams, the nightmares, the occasional memories—do not constitute a sequential temporality. The memory of the chateau does not open up the future but expresses the limitations, and ultimate reifications, of memory.

Flaubert does not use analytical tools to root out the psychological and social causes of his alienation. However, he synthesizes his psychological and social alienation in his dreams and in the evocation of the chateau, which are not "irrealizations" of the past but an expression of the past as "otherness." Nor are they a denial of the past through the romantic pose or the creation, as in the daydreams, of an escapist future. In this sense, they intuit the voice of fiction, that "otherness" which inaugurates a continuity in complete contrast to the false starts, the bad faith, and the fragmentation of this autobiographical enterprise.

The first part of the *Mémoires* is not really memoirs, in that it fails to overcome the solipsism of the alienated voice. The second part of the *Mémoires* optimistically begins with an intersubjective encounter which appears to break the solipsistic impasse and ren-

Les Mémoires d'un fou: The Self and Fiction

der meaningless the fragmentation of time into past, present, and future—that is, the encounter with Maria, in reality Elisa Schlésinger, which plays such an important "figural" role in Flaubert's fiction.

Ironically, having abandoned the *roman intime* at the beginning of his autobiography, Flaubert returns to its first assumption, namely, that falling in love is a totalization of the self in which alienation from time is overcome. Thus, in *Adolphe,* to cite a well-known example, Constant describes love as a temporal synthesis which overcomes the fragmentation of time in what he calls a point of light that unites past and future in an ideal present. Flaubert describes falling in love as a rebirth, the discovery of a new dimension: "C'est que pour la première fois alors, je sentais mon coeur, je sentais quelque chose de mystique, d'étrange comme un sens nouveau. . . . J'étais dans l'étonnement du coeur qui sent sa première pulsation. J'étais comme le premier homme quand il eut connu toutes ses facultés. . . . À quoi je rêvais serait fort impossible à dire; je me sentais nouveau et tout étranger à moi-même; une voix m'était venu dans l'âme" (p. 237). Although this sense of being reborn is accompanied by a feeling of estrangement, the estrangement is one of wonderment rather than alienation. It arises from the consciousness that he has discovered all his faculties. At the same time his new vision mystically transforms material objects into supernatural substances: "Un rien, un pli de sa robe, un sourire, son pied, le moindre mot insignifiant m'impressionnaient comme des choses surnaturelles, et j'avais pur tout un jour à en rêver" (p. 237). As he says, a voice has entered his soul. Not only does it connote the completeness of the self but it overcomes the purely materialistic apprehension of reality that characterizes, throughout the *Mémoires,* the alienated consciousness.

However, this apparent origin of an integrated self and integration between the self and nature proves an illusion. Like the ecstatic reveries of childhood, it has no duration; the voice that appears to rise into consciousness is wordless: "A quoi je rêvais serait fort impossible à dire" (p. 237). Behind the beatific ecstasies of falling in love is physical desire, and physical desire, to Flaubert's mind, means a return to the material opacity of the flesh in which there is no original self at all, only the impulses of a

Les Mémoires d'un fou: The Self and Fiction

determined biological attraction. Thus, from his present perspective, he brutally demystifies the illusion of love: "Deux êtres jetés sur la terre par un hasard, quelque chose, et qui se rencontrent, s'aiment parce que l'un est femme et l'autre homme." Representative of the opacity of this instinct is the language of lovers which falls into the most obvious and self-indulgent clichés: "Les voilà haletant l'un pour l'autre, se promenenant ensemble la nuit et se mouillant à la rosée, regardant le clair de lune et le trouvant diaphane, admirant les étoiles et disant sur tous les tons: 'je t'aime, tu m'aimes, il m'aime, nous nous aimons' " (p. 237). This is not to say that love does not present itself as the most sublime of emotions, but it is, at the same time, "la plus bouffonne des bêtises." From the perspective of demystification he sees through the apparent uniqueness of his feeling for Maria to its commonplace inspiration and expression. He can even describe her through the critical eyes of her detractors: "On aurait pu lui reprocher trop d'embonpoint ou plutôt un negligé artistique. Aussi les femmes en général la trouvaient de mauvais ton" (p. 237). He recognizes in her the fashion of the dark, somewhat masculine woman of the 1830s on the fringe of the bohemian world, who had replaced the "medieval" blondes of an earlier generation. At the same time he recognizes the fashionable, predictable content of their conversation: "On causa littérature, sujet inépuisable avec les femmes."

The high point of Flaubert's intoxication with Maria occurred when they went rowing by moonlight. He was transported not only by her presence but by the setting and the rhythmical movement of the boat and the gentle vibrations of her voice: "Je me plongeais dans mon coeur et j'y trouvais des voluptés infinies" (p. 239). This scene incorporates both the rhythmical sensuousness of the childhood reverie and the harmonious voice of the woman, which in the earlier nightmares were lost in the desperate cry of the drowning mother. The lost unity seems to have been retrieved. The scene recalls a familiar romantic *topos*, that of Lamartine's "Le Lac," for example, or the trip on the lake in Rousseau's *La Nouvelle Héloise*. However, whereas the romantic *topos* was the occasion, in very different ways, in both Rousseau and Lamartine for the sacrifice of sensation, in Flaubert it becomes the occasion for a return to sensation in its most grotesque

Les Mémoires d'un fou: The Self and Fiction

and alienated form. Leaving Maria after the idyllic scene, he imagined her making love to her husband and was overcome by the most extreme rage and jealousy. He returned to his room and recalled once again the rhythms of the ocean and the voice of Maria, but this image was no longer a source of calm or harmony: "J'avais de la lave dans l'âme; j'étais harassé de tout cela et, couché sur le dos, je regardais ma chandelle brûler et son disque trembler au plafond; c'était avec un hébètement stupide que je voyais le suif couler autour du flambeau de cuivre et la flammèche noire s'allonger dans la flamme" (p. 239). He returned to the deadness of pure matter, to the catatonic, empty fixedness on objects that characterized his spleen: time had been reduced to the flow of the tallow down the sides of the candlestick, a masturbatory image that reaffirms Flaubert's demystification of the mystical illusion of his passion for Maria.

In the carriage, as he left the scene where he had known Maria, he recalled every detail, everything that he had seen, felt, said, and done. But it left in him "un chaos, un bourdonnement immense, une folie" (p. 239). Everything had happened as though in a dream. And he returned home to the familiar, hollow, and empty routine.

What disturbs in the evocation of Maria is the fluctuating perspective of the narrator. At one moment he approaches his memories with an almost religious emotion and perceives them as though they are present before his eyes: "J'entends et je vois le frémissement des feuilles, je vois jusqu'au moindre pli de sa robe; j'entends le timbre de sa voix. . ." (p. 236). And he goes on to describe the past in almost hallucinatory detail. At the same time, however, he claims to be an old man looking upon the past from a great distance, whose mocking and demystifying tone is a distortion of the virginity of feeling of the young man. The concrete evocation of the past seems to be an extension of the state of mind of the lover in which every object touched by the beloved comes into being. This is particularly true of the fringed coat which occasioned their meeting. Wandering on the beach, the young boy found the red and black striped coat and pulled it out of reach of the incoming tide. The act was witnessed by Maria, to whom the coat belonged. In his recollection, the coat is no longer merely a useful piece

Les Mémoires d'un fou: The Self and Fiction

of clothing but a particular coat, not classifiable, a singular, concrete reality. To perceive the world with such concreteness, however, means that every object has its discrete reality and that no order between them can be established. Hence, the sense of chaos, an immense swarming, the madness that characterizes Flaubert's first memories of Maria as he returns home. The perspective of the old man, on the other hand, drains these memories of their particularity by analysis and by interpreting a particular experience in terms of general laws. He thus reduces the uniqueness of the young man's experience to a common biological impulse, Maria to a type, and the scene at Trouville to a sociological phenomenon. However, this double perspective was inherent in the original experience. For while it is true that falling in love occasioned the revelation of objects in their particularity, the emergence of forms out of an opaque mass, it was equally characterized by the fall back into matter, into the blinding rage of sexual jealousy, in which, as with the burning candlestick, objects once again retreated into nonbeing.

Flaubert thus finds himself caught between particular, concrete evocations in which he can find no order and a skeptical analysis which interprets every sentimental experience in terms of determined sexual or social impulses. Once again he abandons the *Mémoires,* for the next episode consists of the insertion of a fragment written before he even had the idea of writing his autobiography.[9] As he says, it should be isolated from the rest, and he presents it in its original framework. He portrays himself as an author reading to friends an account of a childish infatuation that preceded his passion for Maria, with a young English girl, Caroline. In his opening remarks he describes to them his authorial perspective: "A l'évocation d'un nom, tous les personnages reviennent, avec leurs costumes et leur langage, jouer leur role comme ils le jouèrent dans ma vie, et je les vois agir devant moi comme un dieu qui regarderait ses mondes crées" (p. 240). Like God, he only has to say a word and the past once again comes into being. But at the same time this God is the director of a play. At his bidding the characters appear on the stage in their costumes and roles. He enjoys being both spectator and manipulator of the scene. Actually, this stance is only a modification of the lived relation between

Les Mémoires d'un fou: The Self and Fiction

himself and those people whom he now calls characters. As he says, they also played roles in his life, implying that there was no authenticity in his interaction with them, only the acting out of some previously determined plot. In life, therefore, he was aware that the role replaced reality and that a fiction replaced the self; but as re-creator of the past he apparently raises himself above the fiction. He has replaced the emtiness of the original role by the powerful, and faintly sadistic, anonymity of the God.

The major role-playing he points to in his anecdote is his own simulation of a grand passion inspired by the plays and novels he has read. Yet his naive feeling for the young girl was not a role, and his re-creation of her frequently belies the manipulative, reifying perspective that he originally claims at the opening of the story. As in his evocation of Maria, he re-creates the lived particularity of the past in which he himself was a total participant: "En passant par une barrière peinte en blanc, son manteau s'accrocha aux épines de la haie; j'allai le détacher, elle me dit merci, avec tant de grâce et de laisser aller que j'en rêvai tout le jour. Puis elles [Caroline and her sister] se mirent à courir, et leurs manteaux, que le vent levait derrière elles, flottaient en ondulant comme un flot qui descend; elles s'arrêtaient essoufflées. Je me rappelle encore leurs haleines qui bruissaient à mes oreilles et qui partaient d'entre leurs dents blanches en vaporeuse fumée" (p. 240). In this scene it is the boy's own emotion that brings into being the particularity of the white gate, the hawthorn bush, the coats of undulating in the wind, objects that would otherwise have remained in their original opacity. So particular and intimate is this memory that he can still hear, he says, the breathing of the two girls. However, he hesitates in his story when it comes to revealing his conversation with Caroline and has one of his friends intrude with "Voilà que tu vas devenir bête" (p. 241), a sentiment with which he hurries to agree, for "le coeur est stupide" (p. 241). He then goes on to show the artificiality, the inauthenticity of the language of the heart, just as he did in the episode of Maria. When he tried to write down his emotion, he reveals, he came out with the most awful, facile, and artificial lines of poetry which he composed in half an hour. He turns his simple feeling for Caroline into a role, into the imitation of romanticism: "Je me battais les

Les Mémoires d'un fou: The Self and Fiction

flancs pour peindre une chaleur que je n'avais vue que dans les livres; puis, à propos de rien, je passais à une mélancolie sombre et digne d'Antony, quoique j'eusse réellement imbibée de candeur et d'un tendre sentiment mêlé de niaiserie, de réminiscences suaves et de parfums de coeur" (p. 241). This skeptical tone infects the rest of the story. He laughs at his naive feeling and subsumes it in a description, a list of the various types of love that correspond to the various stages in a man's life. The concrete and particular evocations of Caroline yield to an abstract classification. This abstraction might be called godlike, and it certainly interprets reality as a sequence of roles, but, as his listeners soon tell him, it is an interruption of the story, an irrelevant digression: " 'Au récit,' demanda un des auditeurs impassible jusque-là, et qui ne quitta sa pipe que pour jeter sur ma digression, qui montait en fumée, la salive de son reproche" (p. 241).

But the narrator is obliged to acknowledge that there is no development in this story: "Il y a une lacune dans l'histoire, un vers de moins dans l'élégie" (p. 241). The images that accurately evoke the sentiment he felt for Caroline are isolated sense impressions that do not make up a story. He had assumed in the beginning that the play was already written: he had only to sit back and watch its unfolding. All he can witness, however, are a few isolated evocations of the past. His digression is an effort to create some kind of temporal development. His listeners are the first to point out that his effort to reduce time to a series of biological impulses—at the age of four one loves horses, the sun, flowers, soldiers; at ten, the little girl one plays with; at thirteen, an ample white breast—is not sufficient to create the development of a story. He can only desultorily sum up the events that did not originate in his own experience. He thus informs his listeners of the facts, what happened to Caroline and her mother, but they hold no more interest than that of gossip or curiosity, and his concluding statement sums up the destiny of his story as well as the destiny of his feeling: "C'est un petit feu qui n'est plus que de la cendre froide" (p. 242).

As in the episode of Maria, Flaubert is caught between the depiction of isolated images that truly re-create the particularity of the past and the caustic analysis of events in terms of reductive

Les Mémoires d'un fou: The Self and Fiction

cause and effect. His failure to create any meaningful temporal sequence in the story of Caroline returns him to that polarity between the infinity of the imagination and the abyss of reality that characterized his first reverie on nature. He expresses this polarity in the distinction between the religious ecstasy inspired by Maria and the sordid experience of the flesh with a prostitute: "Avoir rêvé le ciel et tomber dans la boue" (p. 242). He experiences the flesh as sordid, not out of a puritanical sense of shame but because the fulfillment of desire reduces the expansiveness of his reverie to the physical and temporal contingency of an ejaculation. At the heart of this polarity is Flaubert's failure to extend the ecstatic movement of the reverie in time. He cannot find the appropriate expression for the "poétiques et larges pensées" of the childhood reverie, or for the emergent voice of his reverie on love. After his failure in the anecdotes of Maria and Caroline to transcend the double perspective of the isolated lyrical leap and the reductive, analytical dissection, he returns to a general reflection upon the possibilities and limitations of art.

Although he acknowledges the initial absurdity of wanting to depict man in a block of stone, the soul by words, feelings by sounds, and nature on a varnished canvas, he nevertheless claims that if he has experienced moments of enthusiasm he owes them to art. He throws an interesting light on the nature of this enthusiasm in his description of his reaction to a musical performance: "J'aimais l'orchestre grondant, avec ses flots d'harmonie, ses vibrations sonores et cette vigueur immense qui semble avoir des muscles et qui meurt au bout de l'archet; mon âme suivait la mélodie déployant ses ailes vers l'infini et montant en spirales, pure et lente, comme un parfum vers le ciel. J'aimais le bruit, les diamants qui brillent aux lumières, toutes ces mains de femmes gantées et applaudissant avec des fleurs; je regardais le ballet sautillant, les robes roses ondoyantes; j'écoutais les pas tomber en cadence, je regardais les genoux se détacher mollement avec les tailles penchées" (p. 243). This description combines in miniature the various sources of ecstacy Flaubert has alluded to in previous contexts. It has three distinct articulations: his reaction to the music, to the audience in the theater, and to the dancers on the stage. His aesthetic reaction reproduces the state he himself

Les Mémoires d'un fou: The Self and Fiction

experiences when he is on the edge of creation. It is a soaring flight that is at the same time a melting of boundaries. Overwhelmed by "les flots d'harmonie," he becomes one with the melody that rises in spirals, pure and slow, like a perfume towards the sky. However, he characterizes this aesthetic flight as a spiral, an image that describes his ideal sense of movement and which will be the title of a work he never finished, *La Spirale*.[10] It suggests that the movement away from reality may not in fact be like the flight of a bird or the evaporation of a perfume but made up of different stages, each incorporating and transcending the previous stage. In his plan of *La Spirale* he sketches out a dialectical development between reality and the growing imagination of his hero. Each fantastic state must be, he writes, "la contrepartie exagérée de la réalité et la récompense d'un effort, d'un sacrifice."[11] But this all-important use of the image of the spiral as the model for the structure of a total literary work is only hinted at in Flaubert's description of his aesthetic response to music. It is negated by the natural imagery of the bird and perfume that soar without effort or sacrifice into the sky. Moreover, Flaubert finds an equal ecstasy in the applause of the radiant, bejewelled audience, an image that evokes his own desire for triumph in his schoolday daydreams, the compensation for his failure in the society of his schoolfellows. Finally, both the women in the audience and the sensuous dancers on the stage in their floating dresses provide the origin of a sentimental reverie as did Maria and Caroline. These different ecstasies are fused in their common context, the unreality of the theater itself.

The narrator of the *Mémoires* is somewhat less ecstatic in his reaction to great literary works. Aware of his own failure as a writer, he is envious of the successful writer, as much for the laurels he acquires in life as for his work. Implicit in his envy of those writers who make the crowd "pleurer, gémir, trépigner d'enthousiasme" is his fantasy of revenge and power over the society from which he is estranged. This envy also taints his ultimate rejection of art as the ape of a nameless reality that transcends it.[12] If the highest reality is beyond form and expression, he is in no way inferior, in his own expansive intuitions, to the greatest writers. Thus he returns to his romantic evasion.

Les Mémoires d'un fou: The Self and Fiction

He is caught once again in the problematic of infinity and nothingness. The absence of form means the absence of any limitations and the terrifying intuition into the annihilation of the self. He repeats, however, his apocalyptic desire to dwell in the nothingness that follows the annihilation of men and nature, a nothingness that he can conceive only in terms of the remaining shadows or ashes or drops of water that register the lost earth and sea. The transformation of the ecstatic reverie into the intuition of nothingness was implicit in Flaubert's earliest childhood memories, but it is fused now with the contemptuous hatred of reality that characterized the alienated posturings of the schoolboy faced with the taunting of his materialistic schoolfellows, and the envy of those writers who hold their audience in their hands. Again, in his imagination, he is Nero witnessing the final destruction not only of civilization but of the whole of reality. The correlative of Flaubert's desire for formlessness, which is a desire for a total extinction of the self, is his desire to annihilate man. He immediately follows these reflections by a sadistic attack upon the reader, whom he calls a slave, determined by his base instincts of pride and self-interest.

His reader is no longer the ideal friend, Alfred Le Poittevin, to whom he addresses the manuscript. He has become the bourgeois against whom Flaubert defines his estrangement throughout the *Mémoires*. And, as he elevates his estrangement into a sign of spiritual superiority, and his resentment into sadism, his authorial point of view becomes that of an anonymous God looking down upon the "rotting insects" of humanity. Thus reifying man as the most determined of creatures, Flaubert unwittingly participates in the analytical spirit he claims to abhor. But what separates him from the bourgeois, he believes, what guarantees his essential superiority, is his intuition into the infinite and his urge towards transcendence which the bourgeois explains away by his scientific calculations: "Tu regardes les astres avec un sourire d'orgeuil parce que tu leur as donné des noms et calcules leur distance, comme si tu voulais mesurer l'infini et fermer l'espace dans les bornes de ton esprit. Mais tu te trompes! Qui te dit que, derrière ces mondes de lumière, il n'y en a pas d'autres, infinis encore, et toujours ainsi?" (p. 244). Alienated from men because he intuits an order that defies scientific categories, he is equally alienated

Les Mémoires d'un fou: The Self and Fiction

from art, the forms of which are in inevitable conflict with the formlessness of the infinite. Thus, he concludes that the word is nothing. What he regrets about language, like what he regrets about reality, is its temporality. To quote from *Agonies,* art is nothing: "C'est comme la réalité, une durée."

Nevertheless, he continues to write. He recalls that one summer he returned to the resort where he had met Maria. He found the landscape gray and empty, the places and things, previously transformed by her presence, dull and meaningless. Even the gloomy weather seemed to register her absence. As he contemplated the changed and lifeless scene, he went over in his mind every detail of their encounter and, through these reminiscences, made the extraordinary discovery that he had not loved her in the past. His love was only just beginning in these re-creations of memory: "Comment aurait-elle pu en effet voir que je l'aimais, car je ne l'aimais pas alors, et en tout ce que je vous ai dit, j'ai menti; c'était maintenant que je l'aimais, que je la désirais; que, seul sur le rivage, dans les bois ou dans les champs, je me la créais là, marchant à côté de moi, me parlant, me regardant. Quand je me couchais sur l'herbe, ou que je regardais les herbes ployer sous le vent et la vague battre sur le sable, je pensais à elle, et je reconstruisais dans mon coeur toutes les scènes où elle avait agi, parlé. Ces souvenirs étaient une passion" (p. 246). This new experience has a privileged place in the *Mémoires*, the narrator maintains, with respect to its truthfulness. His previous evocations of Maria were lies. Memory, here, is not a pale and mournful reflection on the past. It originates a willed, hallucinatory vision, a re-creation of Maria in the present. In his interpretation of this episode, Sartre sees a description of the process of fictional "irrealization:" "Rarely has a visionary described with greater depth the process of irrealization." The emergent vision of Maria drains the real Maria of reality, and the visionary Flaubert transcends the frustrations and delimitations of his social self in this simulacrum of the creation of fiction. He describes the nature of this process in a second hallucinatory vision: "Un jour je revenais, vers le crépuscule, je marchais à travers les pâturages couverts de boeufs, je marchais vite, je n'entendais que le bruit de ma marche qui froissait l'herbe; j'avais la tête baissée et je regardais la terre. Ce mouvement régulier m'endormit pour ainsi

Les Mémoires d'un fou: The Self and Fiction

dire, je crus entendre Maria marcher près de moi; elle me tenait le bras et tournait la tête pour me voir, c'était elle qui marchait dans les herbes. Je savais bien que c'était une hallucination que j'animais moi-même, mais je ne pouvais me défendre d'en sourir et je me sentais heureux. Je levai la tête, le temps était sombre; devant moi un magnifique soleil se couchait sous les vagues, on voyait une gerbe de feu s'élever en réseaux, disparaître sous de gros nuages noirs qui roulaient péniblement sur eux, et puis un reflet de ce soleil couchant reparaître plus loin derrière moi, dans un coin de ciel limpide et bleu" (p. 246). This hallucination arises out of the rhythm of walking and the almost hypnotic sleep it induces. The sound of walking is interiorized and reproduced in the imagination as the footsteps of Maria. Flaubert remains well aware that he himself is animating this hallucination, but it nevertheless produces in him a sense of pleasure. This experience, then, is not the reproduction of a past experience but the creation of an image in the present. It is above all characterized by sound and movement. The rhythm of walking itself instigates the created image, and Flaubert experiences the image of Maria as movement. The movement is continuous, in process. Thus, in the use of the imperfect that will predominate in his later novels, he describes her as she was walking, as she was turning her head to look at him. This temporality is no longer the "empty duration" that he labelled language; it is the joyous experience of the self in a temporal modality. Nor, as in his previous memories, is he overwhelmed or possessed by the image. He is not a passive observer or a detached manipulator, as he tried to be in his story of Caroline. He is both creator of the image and created in it. What Flaubert wrote to Taine, many years after writing the *Mémoires*, about the difference between pathological and poetic hallucination clearly indicates the "poetic" character of his hallucination of Maria: "Dans l'hallucination proprement dite, il y a toujours terreur; vous sentez que votre personnalité vous echappe; on croit que l'on va mourir. Dans la vision poétique, au contraire, il y a joie; c'est quelque chose qui entre en vous."[13] This poetic vision is only the first stage of the creative process, but it marks a necessary first step.

Although Sartre acknowledges that this hallucinatory vision

Les Mémoires d'un fou: The Self and Fiction

demarcates a transition from reality to the imagination, his use of the word "irrealization" to describe the process has a basically pejorative overtone. He suggests the identity between Flaubert's imaginative modality and an incapacity for the successful accomplishment of real experience. Fiction therefore becomes a compensation or a way out of an unresolved dilemma. He thus concludes from Flaubert's description of his hallucination of Maria that "true love, for Gustave, can only be an imaginary sentiment."[14] He further implies the narcissism of Flaubert's imagination by stressing the narcissistic content of the hallucination: Flaubert narcissistically doubles himself in the image of the woman for whom he becomes a passive object, his head bent to the ground, the self-absorbed focus of her gaze. Sartre goes so far as to liken the hallucination to a masturbatory image: "It would be more accurate to speak of a masturbatory schema. In this case, as we know, the image is the diaphanous mediation between masturbator and masturbated."[15] A footnote by Sartre referring to Flaubert's attitude to Louise Colet further confirms the pejorative intentionality of this interpretation: "The same thing also applies to desire properly speaking: he will prefer to masturbate over the beautiful slippers of Louise while evoking the beautiful body of the Muse than actually sleep with her. And this is also the explanation for his perpetual postponements of their meetings."[16]

Thus, from this perspective the hallucination of Maria is of the same kind as Flaubert's masturbatory images inspired by the shoe of Louise Colet. It indicates a pathological preference for the image over reality. It is important, however, to make a radical distinction between the masturbatory and the poetic image. Flaubert himself has described the intentionality of the masturbatory image in his description of the aftermath of the *partie de barque,* when, obsessed by images of Maria in the arms of her husband, he returned to his room. He experienced this imagery as a harassment, and it produced in him a catatonic "hébètement" in which time was reduced to the most opaque immobility of dripping wax. The correlative of the imagery was the deadness of the objects of his perception. Similarly, Louise's shoe expresses both the reification of the woman and the deadness of the masturbatory fantasy which itself reifies the masturbator. This is obviously not the

Les Mémoires d'un fou: The Self and Fiction

case with Flaubert's hallucination of Maria. Sartre's notion of irrealization implies that creation means the irrealization of life. While it may be true that Flaubert continually distances himself from the "active life," his creative imagination names the beginning of experience on another level, irreducible to the first.

Unlike his childhood reveries on nature, romantic daydreams, or nightmares, Flaubert's hallucination of Maria does not describe an abortive sense of the infinite, compensatory images of success and revenge, or the terror of the loss of the self, but the experience of self in a temporal dimension through the creation of the image. Form is no longer the sign of a limitation but the means towards self-creation. It is no longer a question of trying to express the infinite or of reducing man to material causes. The soul and body are no longer in irreconcilable opposition. The rhythm of walking may occasion the liberation of the image but cannot be said to cause it. Cause and effect are absorbed into simultaneity.

Although Flaubert's hallucination of Maria describes the origin of a fictional consciousness, its destiny is problematical. When the hallucination faded, he recalls, he became aware that the sun was disappearing behind the clouds, leaving only a reflection in the corner of the sky. He continued walking towards the sea. By the time he reached the coast, the sun was half sunk into the sea, while its reflection in the sky was growing paler and paler. As he contemplated this sunset, he recalled yet another he had once seen while riding along the coast when, mesmerized by the action of the waves and the movement of the stones under his horse's hooves, he had suddenly become aware of the uncanny effect left by the sun which had dropped beneath the waves leaving behind a somber color, as though something black had hovered over the scene, a threatening shadow relieved only by the white wings of the gulls against the dark water and the white foam lapping against the rocks. Not only does the hallucination of Maria mean an interruption of the conventional experience of time, the end of the hallucination inaugurates a sense of death, strangeness and the uncanny. In fact, the second image of the horseman riding along the coast describes the movement from absorption in rhythmical movement to the frightening rediscovery of reality. Flaubert flees the consequences of this insight that the experience of

Les Mémoires d'un fou: The Self and Fiction

the imagination seems to embody the experience of a death, and in the final pages of the *Mémoires* rejects language altogether for failing to *imitate* a preexistent reality. This flight is marked by a lapse into romantic and sentimental banality: "Pouvez-vous dire par des mots le battement du coeur? pouvez-vous dire une larme et peindre son cristal humide qui baigne l'oeil d'une amoureuse langueur? pouvez-vous dire tout ce que vous ressentez en un jour? " (p. 247).

Since language cannot reproduce reality, then, he concludes, no authentic language is possible and his *Mémoires*, as the effort to discover an authentic language of the self, must fail. But the failure of the *Mémoires* is rather Flaubert's failure to accept the constitutive possibilities of language. At the end of the first part, he refers to memory as a reflection of the setting sun; at the end of the second, the same image returns and connotes a more drastic sacrifice of immediate reality in the name of fiction. Unwilling to make the leap from memoirs to fiction, he once again assumes the romantic mask he had originally wished to shed. And his final words sum up the various kinds of false consciousness that dominate the work: regret for the impossibility of the physical possession of Maria, regret for the absence of the infinite, self-pity, and contempt for reality. He reduces time to the indiscriminate ringing of the church bells, a meaningless death knell. Thus, he remains faithrul to his madness by returning to his original point of departure. His *Mémoires* finally describes a vicious circle.

NOTES

1. For a detailed analysis of Flaubert's reading matter between 1835 and 1842, see Jean Bruneau's *Les Débuts littéraires de Gustave Flaubert* (Paris, 1962), chap. 11.
2. Flaubert, *Oeuvres complites*, Éditions du Seuil (Paris, 1964), p. 91. All page references throughout this and subsequent chapters will be to this text.
3. Ibid., p. 103.
4. This breakthrough into autobiography does not mean that Flaubert has definitively abandoned the grotesque tale. After the

Les Mémoires d'un fou: The Self and Fiction

Mémoires he will write another skeptical horror story in the old mode, "Les Funerailles du docteur Mathurin" (1839).

5. He writes to Le Poittevin on 11 October 1838: "Je suis à moitié des *Confessions* de Jean-Jacques Rousseau. C'est admirable. Voilà la vraie école de style."
6. In his *Flaubert und seine "Versuchung des Heiligen Antonius"* (Minden, 1912), Theodor Reik uses the dreams of the *Mémoires* to reveal the source of the neurotic patterns found throughout his work. However, such a procedure is incapable of making a distinction between the dreams as they appear in the *Mémoires* and, for example, the visions of the *Tentation de saint Antoine*. It cannot account for the change of significance effected upon a common material by a change of context.
7. Translated from Jean-Paul Sartre, *L'Idiot de la famille* (Paris, 1971), vol. 2, p. 1543.
8. Ibid., p. 1529.
9. That the insertion was in fact composed before the rest of the work is strongly suggested by the state of the (now displaced) manuscript (NAF 23.839, 141, recto). René Descharmes describes it thus: "Up to the end of chapter XV, it is very easy to make out additions and corrections to the first draft of the fragment; when he wished to insert the episode of Gertrude Collier into his narrative, he had to contrive the transitions—and they remain quite crude—and create some link between ideas: these necessities of composition can be observed, by an examination of the manuscript, in obvious differences of an external nature. These pages are of a different kind of paper, smaller and yellower, than those which precede and follow them."
10. See E. W. Fischer, *"Un inédit de Gustave Flaubert: La Spirale,"* La *Table ronde,* avril 1958, pp. 96–124.
11. Ibid., p. 96.
12. The ideal language, for Flaubert, would be able to modify reality. In *Smahr* he imagines a language which would have an immediate effect upon desire: ". . . une page enfin, que, si elle était affichée sur les murs, mettrait les murs en chaleur eux-mêmes, et ferait courir les populations dans les lupanars devenus désormais trop petits, et forcerait hommes et femmes à s'accoupler dans la rue. . ." (p. 211).
13. *Corresp.* 5.951 (1968), (A Hippolyte Taine).
14. *L'Idiot de la famille,* 2.1528.
15. Ibid., p. 1528.
16. Ibid.

3

Novembre:
The Failure of the Lyrical Autobiography

Flaubert composed *Novembre* between autumn 1840 and autumn 1842 during the difficult years he spent as a law student in Paris. It marks a return to the autobiographical genre of the *Mémoires*. Trapped in a vicious circle of personal reminiscence, he left the *Mémoires* to write *Smahr* (1839), a mystery play about man's relation to the cosmos and his desire for the infinite. Despite this universal treatment of what were originally very private perceptions, he still felt that he had failed to create distance on himself. The distortions and "poetic" effusions of an inadequately objective spontaneity everywhere betrayed him and, like the madman of the *Mémoires*, he finally abandoned language as inadequate.

Novembre, however, is a new point of departure for Flaubert. Although he returns to the form of a personal autobiography, he no longer desires to be the vessel of poetic spontaneity but the laborer of language who would turn his lyricism into a viable literary expression through the elaboration of a *style*. His intention is not to write down everything as it comes into his head but to subsume his autobiographical material—much of which recapitulates that of the *Mémoires*—in a unified voice. Thus, *Novembre* seems to have resolved the profound ambiguities and confusions of the *Mémoires*. Instead of wondering whether he is author or character and whether he is a madman, he chooses to be an author

Novembre: The Failure of the Lyrical Autobiography

who can separate himself from his fictional narrator.

The opening tonality of *Novembre* is that of the *roman intime,* of *Werther, Adolphe,* and *René.* Although the narrator is sad, he rests in his sadness, as though it were only one of the seasons, part of a harmonious and necessary cosmic rhythm. Whereas the narrator of the *Mémoires* established from the beginning that his consciousness was divided, the narrator of *Novembre* establishes a unity of perspective through an elegiac lyricism which consists in making an equation between the mind and nature. "Flaubert's essential debt," Jean Bruneau writes of *Novembre,* "is the profound harmony between state of mind and landscape, between the human soul and nature, revealed to him by the masters of romantic writers, Rousseau and Chateaubriand."[1]

The narrator loves autumn, he announces at the beginning of the work, because it goes well with remembering. And he will continually make such correspondences between his state of mind and the seasons. His spirits revive with the spring, his sensuality with the summer, and so on. If the mind reflects nature, then its relation to the events of its past should not be one of dissociation and crisis, as was the case in the *Mémoires,* but one of continuity. Thus, even though the narrator of *Novembre* looks at his dead past with horror and irony, in comparing it to the dead leaves, his horror to the coming winter, and his irony to the antics of the wind, he situates himself not in a desperate void but in a natural unity: "L'amer parfum des jours qui ne sont plus m'est revenu, avec l'odeur de l'herbe sèche et des bois morts; mes pauvres années ont passé devant moi, comme emportées par l'hiver dans une tourmente lamentable; quelque chose de terrible les roulait dans mon souvenir, avec plus de furie que la brise ne faisait courir les feuilles dans les sentiers paisibles; une ironie étrange les frôlait et les retournait pour mon spectacle, et puis toutes s'envolaient ensemble et se perdaient dans un ciel morne" (p. 248). The past may have died, but he remains as present as the sullen sky that has absorbed the dead leaves.

However, he immediately goes on to elaborate his relation to the past by the use of another metaphor which threatens the analogy between the mind and nature. He compares himself to an old man visiting the catacombs and his past to the rows and

Novembre: The Failure of the Lyrical Autobiography

rows of the dead. The cyclical time of nature in which his mind was the hub has turned into spleen in which both time and the mind are frozen in an endless void. There is no possibility of subsuming the past in a present unity, or of a future renewal; all that remains is the debris of "a thousand past existences."[2] The dissociated voice of the *Mémoires* has broken through the original elegiac tones of *Novembre.* This note of discord, however, reveals the fragility of the analogy between mind and nature and will become an integral part of the work. No matter how much he might wish to be one with nature, the narrator constantly finds himself thrown back upon an unassimilable subjectivity which he experiences as empty estrangement. Nevertheless, Flaubert persistently returns to the language of natural analogy in an effort to reconstitute a unified perspective.

In the *Mémoires* the necessary correlative to the madman's estrangement from himself was his estrangement from other men. Although he initially addressed himself to one ideal reader, this reader rapidly turned into the incarnation of "the others," the bourgeois enemy. In *Novembre,* on the other hand, as a correlative to the narrator's elegiac relation to his past is his intimate confidence in his reader, who is not the stranger in the street or the anonymous member of society who is impervious to his dreams but the mirror of himself, someone who has experienced the same feelings. Even his increasing discouragement does not immediately lead him to negate his identification with the reader; he supposes that his withdrawal into himself is something all men know. Thus, it is from the standpoint not of estrangement but unity that the narrator summons up his past.

Significantly, his favorite memories are less of events than of daydreams which, in their inwardness and projections of a future fulfillment, negate the emptiness of his actual experience. In recalling his years at school, the misery is blotted out by a vision of what life would be like at twenty. As he sat at his desk, he imagined the future as a synthesis of exquisite sound, light, and perfume, the scene from a fairy story in which room opened upon room, in which diamonds sparkled in the light of chandeliers, and where doors, at a magic word, would reveal magnificent and rapturous perspectives. The content of his daydreams reveals their

Novembre: The Failure of the Lyrical Autobiography

purpose; they aimed for ecstasy, transcendence, and eternal unity. The key image of this transcendence is woman, who, even when he recalls an experience and not a daydream, is resplendently illuminated.

The more distant the woman, the better she embodied a transcendent ecstasy. He had only to say the word "mistress," to imagine an infinite world of forbidden pleasures. He adored the tight-rope walker in her sequined costume, literally above him and close to the source of light as she walked between the lamps hung in the trees. But it was the actress who most fully represented the ideal. She came into being only on the stage, in the brightly illuminated world created for her by a poet. Even the men who shared his admiration for the mistress, the acrobat, and the actress were not, as was the husband of Maria in the *Mémoires,* a source of jealousy and rage but a further substantiation of the value of the ideal image. For such women, he observes, kings conquer and ruin themselves; for such women, craftsmen labor and workmen mine gold and chip marble. Acquisition and the worship of gold, equated with the decadence of bourgeois society in the *Mémoires,* are absorbed into homage to the ideal, like the flowers and other tributes thrown at the feet of the actress. Thus, the painful sense of mediation and social alienation that pervades the *Mémoires* is negated in the name of a transforming and unifying transcendence. Nor did he anticipate that his awakening sensuality would dispel the dazzling visions of childhood. He felt that in entering real life he was entering an immense harmony "où mon coeur chantait un hymne et vibrait magnifiquement" (p. 251).

However, as he became physically capable of fulfilling desire, he paradoxically fled women. Instead of experiencing passion, he studied it in books and fuelled his imagination with accounts of extreme sensuality, violence, destruction, and the extraordinary profusions of nature. But what finite satisfaction could still all this teeming desire? And this implied question ironically reversed all the hopes of his endless daydreams. The gateway to the ideal turned to a giant anthill into which he had stepped, and his idealism to an immense bitterness, what he calls the synthesis and the irony of a life only *apparently* full of movement and variety. Still, he moved even further away from experience in the world and

Novembre: The Failure of the Lyrical Autobiography

plunged more deeply into the imagination.

Seeking an ecstatic fusion with nature, he imagined he was a bee, flying freely in a limitless universe, deciphering voices no other ear could understand and feasting on divine harmonies. With the clouds and sun he recalls, he composed pictures that defied representation in any other language, and had lightning flashes of insight into the mysteries of human behavior. Thus, to use his imagery, by means of this art without a canvas, this poetry without words, he soared once again into the realm of the ideal, no longer a simple bee but an eagle, proud and solitary, with an inevitable disgust for earthly things. Although he persisted in his flights of fancy, he became increasingly aware of their correlative, his dissociation from reality and overwhelming ennui. When his spiralling eagle flights collapsed, as was inevitable, he experienced reality as a meaningless whirlwind in which people passed like ghosts or like shop signs from the perspective of a passing carriage.[3] The emotional wholeness projected by his fantasies—that seamless unity between himself and nature—was flatly contradicted by the living death of his experience of himself in the world.

At this point, the narrator begins to wonder about the authenticity of his lyrical voice. His poetic rhapsodies may have been only the memories of second-rate literature, inflated figures of speech, the aim of which was to disguise his lack of passion or feeling. He may have imitated a romantic style, but he had no emotional substance: "Ce n'était point la douleur de René, ni l'immensité céleste de ses ennuis, plus beaux et plus argentés que les rayons de la lune; je n'étais point chaste comme Werther ni débauché comme Don Juan; je n'étais, pour tout, ni assez pur ni assez fort" (p. 252). He was no romantic hero whose passions raised him above the common run, but an ordinary man of his time, caught in an alienated routine. Although, he acknowledges, when he began writing he found his language beautiful, he can see no point in continuing the same mournful dirge which, he says, evokes his tears and threatens to stifle his voice.

When the narrator thus questions his language on the grounds that it lacks an authentic emotional source, he stops being a character, a Werther, or a René, and shows himself as Flaubert, the troubled author who had wished, in *Novembre,* to transcend,

Novembre: The Failure of the Lyrical Autobiography

through the creation of authorial distance and the elaboration of a style, the problems of personal authenticity and estrangement which had formed the subject matter of the *Mémoires.* Nevertheless, he continues writing. Clearly, it is not the passionate dynamism of a romantic character which moves the action along; rather, the raison d'être of the work resides in the dynamic interplay between flight of fantasy and fall into reality. Each extreme unleashes its dialectical opposite—as fancy unleashes ennui, ennui grief—thus creating a basis for dynamic continuity. No matter how self-indulgent, the narrator's grief that he cannot grieve dissipates his detachment and estrangement and reestablishes the tone of elegiac harmony. He thus leaves his present wintry mood to evoke not past daydreams but happy memories.

In contrast to the vaporousness of his fancy, the narrator's memories refer to a lived reality. However, that reality is drenched with inwardness, intimacy, and shared harmony. It no longer appears to be a fallen, alienated state but is fused with the qualities of the imagination. "Let us recall the happy days," he begins, "when we were many, when the sun shone, when the hidden birds sang after the rain, when we went walking in the garden; the paths were wet, the rose petals had fallen on to the ground, the air was full of perfume." This description of the garden both embodies the movement in the text from grief to memory and incorporates the reflective interiority of remembering. In spite of the sun, the beauty of the scene is subdued and bears the marks of recent rain: birds have hidden and petals have fallen; pathways are still wet. It is suffused with the regret that in the midst of happiness he had not been fully capable of enjoying it, had not savored each minute of it so that it might have passed more slowly. His memories overcome his solitude and estrangement both through the evocation of community of feeling and through intensity of sensation. Thus, he recalls one afternoon when he and his friends toasted their bread over the stove and chatted about what they had seen at the theater, whom they might fall in love with, and what they would do when they left school; and another occasion when, lying in the grass, he looked at the sun through his interlaced fingers and watched the interplay of light, and then closed his eyes to experience even more intense patches of color under his lids. These

Novembre: The Failure of the Lyrical Autobiography

memories are remarkable for both the absence of the inflation and insubstantiality which characterized his evasive daydreams and of the irony, disgust, and estrangement which characterized his return to reality. It therefore seems surprising that they should produce such a dizzying anxiety in the narrator, a sickening sense that there is no connection between who he was and who he is: "Comme tout cela est loin! Est-ce que je vivais dans ce temps-là, était-ce bien moi? est-ce moi maintenant? Chaque minute de ma vie se trouve tout à coup séparée de l'autre par un abîme, entre hier et aujourd'hui il y a pour moi une éternité qui m'épouvante. . . ." (p. 253). It is not just a question of not recognizing the boy in his memories but of acknowledging that there is a terrifying eternity, an abyss, between the minutes of his existence.

Such existential anxiety is a long way from Flaubert's original intention to incorporate the past within a cyclical natural harmony. And it is precisely his puncturing of his rhetorical excesses and distorting irony, his creation of an uninflated language, that reveal the temporality of consciousness. Through identification with nature, through daydream and ennui, his narrator had fled consciousness of death. In reconstituting concrete moments of his past, he experiences his constitutive self for whom to create is at the same time to die to the past and participate in the passing of time.

Although his memories do not provide the sheltering harmony he had sought in them, they give him greater insight into the relation between his evasive fantasies and reality. His fantasies, he admits, were based on desires that had no object and melancholy that had no cause—or so many objects and so many causes that no single one could satisfy or explain them. As they proliferated, his capacity for action shrank. He was merely the passive scene for passions which, finding no possiblity of concrete expression, struggled for space and enflamed one another as though through concentric mirrors. He recognizes that there was little correlation between what he wanted to be and what he was: modest in reality, his fantasies were full of pride; he lived in solitude and dreamt of glory; he was withdrawn from the world but dreamt of shining in society; he was chaste but abandoned himself in his dreams to unbridled sensuality. This tension between the elaborate wealth and proliferation of his fantasies and the poverty of his experience

Novembre: The Failure of the Lyrical Autobiography

and his expression of them reached a climax in mad fits in which his senses seemed to explode and he imagined he contained a divine incarnation, that he would give birth to a God: "Tenté par toutes les voluptés de la pensée, aspirant à moi toutes les poésies, toutes les harmonies, et écrasé sous le poids de mon coeur et de mon orgueil, je tombais anéanti dans un abîme de douleurs, le sang me fouettait la figure, mes artères m'étourdissaient, ma poitrine semblait rompre, je ne voyais plus rien, je ne sentais plus rien, j'étais ivre, j'étais fou, je m'imaginais être grand, je m'imaginais contenir une incarnation suprême, dont la révélation eût émerveillé le monde, et ses déchirements, c'était la vie même de dieu que je portais dans mes entrailles" (p. 253).[4]

In recalling these extremes, he becomes more conscious of the relation between fantasy and estrangement: the very boundlessness, the formlessness of his desires and dreams, which he had equated with the boundlessness of God, were disguises for a vast emptiness. And he admits that, far from sheltering an imminent God, he is, to use his metaphor, an empty temple where thistles grow among the stones and owls build their nests in the crumbling pillars. Showing a Baudelairean flair for images of spleen and reification, he thus reverses the romantic use of natural imagery with which he began *Novembre.* The stones, the vegetation, the birds, are not signs of enduring or vital life but symbols of decline and death. He does not transcend himself through elegiac contemplation of the ruin, a common romantic *topos,* the ruin is himself. In a second image, he compares his seething fantasies, what he calls "the variety of his being," to a tropical forest: "L'azur est rempli de parfums et de poisons, les tigres bondissent, les éléphants marchent fièrement comme des pagodes vivantes, les dieux mystérieux et difformes sont cachés dans les creux des cavernes parmi de grands monceaux d'or; et, au milieu, coule le large fleuve, avec des crocodiles béants qui font claquer leurs écailles dans le lotus du rivage, et ses îles de fleurs que le courant entraîne avec des troncs d'arbre et des cadavres verdis de la peste" (p. 253). This parnassian, decadent and paradoxical landscape in which perfume mingles with poison, gods are misshapen, crocodiles swim among lotus blossoms, and the river drags along both flowers and pestiferous corpses, undermines, as in the symbol of the empty temple,

Novembre: The Failure of the Lyrical Autobiography

the lyrical conception of nature on which *Novembre* is based. Once again, nature is not an all embracing unity with which the mind can establish a transcendent harmony, it is divided, both beautiful and evil. And it is no longer re-created as an external reality, like the initial autumnal scene of *Novembre,* but as a metaphor for the mind itself. Finding such symbolic expression for his emptiness and feverish imagination, the narrator briefly escapes the wordlessness of that excess of idealism which deluded him into thinking that he contained a God and reduced him, in fact, to matter, to the violence of blood, arteries and lungs.[5]

However, the result of this demystification of his illusions of divine creativity is nostalgia for the infinite and contempt for the monotonous routine of everyday existence. Dwelling on the bourgeois destiny which threatened and threatens him, he turns his contempt upon the reader—hitherto regarded as another self—and berates him as the incarnation of the bourgeois, that alien other, smugly self-satisfied, sure of himself and his success. The intensity of his hatred and the violence of his invective—the bourgeois are scoundrels, cowards, idiots and eye-sores—suggest that the bourgeois is not so much the hated other as the hated image of himself. No longer believing that he is a born genius, he sees himself condemned to the mechanical routine of a mere copyist. Veering from one extreme to another, he nevertheless persists in his conception of the writer as a passive receptacle: both the divinely inspired genius and the bureaucratic scribbler write from an authoritative dictation. Thus he reaches an impasse. He looks back at his past and sees only a great void. Even his love of nature, the original source of his lyricism and of a possible plenitude, had proved insubstantial: "J'avais pris le soleil en haine, j'étais excédé du bruit des fleuves, de la vue des bois, rien ne me semblait sot comme la campagne; tout s'assombrit et se rapetissa, je vecus dans un crépuscule perpétuel" (p. 255). Incapable of constituting any future, incapable any longer of believing in the lyrical relation between himself and nature, he recalls his darkest memory, his thoughts on suicide. However, having decided to kill himself, random, vivid, and concrete memories—of his dog, of clothes he had worn—each stimulating another, suddenly illuminated the darkness. And, as in the past they broke through an impasse, these

Novembre: The Failure of the Lyrical Autobiography

memories have the effect of shattering the impasse of the present.

Having negated time by longing for the infinite, by equating it with mechanical routine, and by desiring death, he enters it again. Once again, the vivid, concrete images of his past have made him aware of the anxiety of what he calls the absolute loss of the past which always accompanies remembering. Reflecting that one can sometimes spend centuries in thinking of a certain hour which will never return, which is in nothingness forever, and which one would buy back at the cost of all the future, he perceives with great intensity that, rather than arresting time, memory heightens his sense of the irrevocability of its passing. The greater the effort to reconstitute the past—the centuries spent on the recollection of a single hour—the greater the sense of its receding into nothing. Nevertheless, memories are like bright torches in a dark room. They light up objects only within their immediate vicinity, but without them everything would be in darkness. It is in this context that the narrator recalls the most brilliant memory of his past, an epiphany which he experienced while walking, one day, towards X (Trouville).

As Jean Bruneau has pointed out, this experience takes on archetypal proportions in the work of Flaubert; it reappears, assuming different meanings in different contexts, in the first *Éducation sentimentale, Par les Champs et par les grèves,* and the *Tentation de saint Antoine.* Like the hallucination described in the last pages of the *Mémoires,* it began when he lost himself, the narrator recalls, in the cadence of walking. His footsteps had seemed to lull his thought to sleep, and all he was aware of was their sound and movement. When he came to himself, he was on a plateau, in a ploughed field, facing the brilliantly blue sea. As the sun beat down upon it, he found himself absorbed in a transcendent natural unity: "Le soleil répandait dessus une profusion de perles lumineuses; des sillons de feu s'étendaient sur les flots; entre le ciel azuré et la mer plus foncée, l'horizon rayonnait, flamboyait; la voûte commençait sur ma tête et s'abaissait derrière les flots, qui remontaient vers elle, faisant comme le cercle d'un infini invisible. Je me suis couché dans un sillon et j'ai regardé le ciel, perdu dans la contemplation de sa beauté" (p. 256). The unifying element is primarily light. The sea is suffused with a profu-

Novembre: The Failure of the Lyrical Autobiography

sion of "luminous pearls" and "streams of fire," and the boundary between sea and sky is blurred in the flames of the horizon. His head seemed to be the cornerstone of a vault embracing sky and sea like the circle of an "invisible infinite." Lying down in one of the ploughed furrows, he literally sank himself more deeply into the natural unity and lost himself in contemplation of its beauty.

Flaubert creates the effect of unity by establishing correspondence between the elements. Thus "perles lumineuses" and "sillons de feu" refer equally to fire and water, to light and sea. Moreover, the word "sillon" occurs in another of its meanings to describe the furrow of earth. As his narrator established himself in the literal *sillon*, Flaubert establishes himself in the suggestive and multivalent word which unifies his imagery. Other correspondences are effected by the use of synesthesia, as when he refers to the *sound* of the sun: "Le soleil lui-même semblait avoir son bruit." And sound, like light, becomes a means of creating harmony—responses are set up between the sound of the sun, of the waves, and of quail *circling* overhead.

As the narrator sank more deeply into the experience, it grew more intimately sensual: "L'odeur des vagues montait jusqu'à moi, avec la senteur du varech et des plantes marines; quelquefois elles paraissaient s'arrêter ou venaient mourir sans bruit sur le rivage festonné d'écume, comme une lèvre dont le baiser ne sonne point. Alors dans le silence de deux vagues, pendant que l'Océan gonflé se taisait, j'écoutai le chant de cailles un instant, puis le bruit des flots recommençait, et après, celui des oiseaux" (p. 256). He became aware of the tangy smell of seaweed and sea plants, of the rhythms of the swollen ocean as it came in to embrace the shore, and most intimately of all, of the silence between waves. The progression of the imagery from light to sound to smell to touch to a silence as immediate as suspended breath effects a transition from a contemplated unity—the focus of which is light and sky—to a sensual unity—the focus of which is sea and earth. From being an infinite invisible, nature becomes a breathing and anthropomorphized reality. This double image is maintained in the next phase of the ecstatic experience when the narrator, filled, as he says, with the spirit of God and an intense sense of adoration,

Novembre: The Failure of the Lyrical Autobiography

ran down to the sea. He found the presence of God both in the immensity of light and azure and in the waves which swirled intimately about his feet and embraced the rocks with their "bras liquides."

The retreating sea had left its exquisite tracks—again, the word "sillon"—on the shore, and he read in them the sign of a perfect harmony, both aesthetic and moral, that can be perceived only in moments of great ecstasy. Since there could be nothing discordant in nature, there could be nothing evil; it was both beautiful and good. However, with this insight, his ecstatic vision of nature began to fade. Instead of feeling a perfect rapport between himself and nature, a perfect understanding and love, he became unpleasantly aware of the sharpness of the stones under his feet and the hardness of the rocks against his hands, of nature's *indifference*. And he replaced his fading pantheistic experience with a celebration of Christianity: "Et je songeais alors combien il était doux de chanter le soir, à genoux, des cantiques au pied d'une madone qui brille aux candélabres, et d'aimer la Vierge Marie, qui apparait aux marins, dans un coin du ciel, tenant le doux enfant Jésus dans ses bras" (p. 257). However, this did not succeed in maintaining the religious ecstasy; he found himself overtaken once again by malediction. Life had returned to him, he says, through the feeling of suffering. He was reentering humanity.

Returning to the scene on his way back from X later the same day, he found only the most meaningless physical traces of his experience, footprints on the sand, the depression left in the grass by his body. Once more he was struck by the lack of continuity between past and present. In a single day he had lived two separate existences, the second of which already consisted only of memories of the first. He had passed within a few hours from an experience of the greatest plenitude to one of the keenest loss.

The movement of this entire episode is extremely important in the understanding of *Novembre*. To begin with, it is prompted by the physical rhythms of walking which produce a semisomnolent state of mind and liberate the self from contingent preoccupations. In this state, the narrator of the *Mémoires* is opened up to the imagined presence of Maria, the narrator of *Novembre,* to the rhythms of nature. The strength of these rhythms and his recep-

Novembre: The Failure of the Lyrical Autobiography

tivity combine to make him feel that he is part of the whole. Nature subsumes him, at first in the brilliant light which, as shown by his earlier daydreams, always stood for transcendence, and then in the sensual embrace of earth and sea. Thus, it is not only the perfect interplay of natural forms and forces that leads him to the high point of his ecstasy—the recognition of the presence of aesthetic and moral perfection, of God, in nature—but the negation of himself as a discordant and unassimilated element in the universal design. His sense of unity with nature is primarily dependent on his physical fusion with it (and he both presses himself into the earth and enters the sea). His aesthetic and moral *insight,* however, has the inevitable effect of distancing him from that physical intimacy. Just as the delicate traces on the shore register the absence of the tide, his observations on the significance of these signs register a withdrawal from his immersion in the natural plenitude. At this moment nature becomes alien and indifferent, and because of its indifference, as hard as the stones under his feet and as resistant as the rocks against his hands.

The transition from the pantheistic ecstasy to the Christian reverie is an abrupt and disturbing one. The alien indifference of nature to man destroys the narrator's sense of being embraced in a divine love but does not necessarily lead to the adoration of the Virgin which immediately follows. Moreover, the language of the reverie has the naive and sentimentalized simplicity of an Épinal engraving illustrating a child's book on Christ, and the static and rigid character of its imagery contrasts sharply with the dynamic flow of the previous description. Such awkwardness represents here a flight from the perception of discord and disunity. With the image of Mary, the narrator projects another embodiment of a loving presence and emotionally transposes himself into the enraptured child at the foot of the madonna, and the baby in her arms. He thus protects himself from the indifference of nature as sailors protect themselves from shipwreck. Immersion in nature now means only death and destruction. The image of divine mother and child proves, however, very fragile shelter. Projected as a means of gratification, it is symbiotically attached to the narrator's wishes and offers him no guarantee of its substantial and objective truth. Inevitably, like a dream, it fades away.

Novembre: The Failure of the Lyrical Autobiography

The collapse of the pantheistic episode returns the narrator to a keener awareness of his separation from nature. His desire for a transcendent absorption in a loving presence disintegrates into the fear of annihilation by purely destructive matter. Even the acknowledgment that there is a perfect formal and moral harmony in nature leaves him painfully aware that, as a reflective being, he remains outside of it. Significantly, the episode closes with a reflection on memory, the anxious temporal modality, which reveals to him the dizzying rift between immersion in sensuous experience and consciousness. Once again the precarious unity on which *Novembre* is based—the identification between mind and nature—is radically undermined. In a typical reversal, however, the narrator leaves his reflection on memory to recollect its opposite, the immediate experience of desire.

What remained undeniable about nature, even if he had to abandon the idea that it was animated by a loving and purely good God, was its physical dynamism. Thus, even though, as earlier, he compares his frustrated passions to a prison confining him within an endless, constricted circle, he does not suppose that the excess of his frustration proved that he was about to incarnate God. On the contrary, he acknowledges its physical, uniquely material source. On this level, he could again identify himself with nature because his body harmoniously follows the natural (physical) laws of birth, growth, and death. Like the Baudelaire of "La Charogne," he accepts ugliness and decay as an integral part of this natural process. One day, oppressed by his passions and the summer heat of the city, he found himself mesmerized by the sight of a "golden wheel" of flies swarming around a piece of rotting flesh, and longed to be similarly transported above the deadness of his existence. The transfigured ugliness of the flies becomes an image for the possibility of a transcendence *d'en bas.*

Thus, he recalls, he abandoned his idealism and indulged his sensuality, "a river furiously overflowing its banks and drowning his heart in torrents more tumultuous and vertiginous than those of the mountains." He looked for a human shape in the soft clouds that seemed to weigh upon his body, and in the folds and hollows of the waves. Desire seemed to exude from his pores, and, in the absence of any external satisfaction, he sought it in

Novembre: The Failure of the Lyrical Autobiography

narcissistic caresses. He longed to press something in his arms and stifle it in his own heat, or else "me dédoubler moi-même, aimer cet être et nous fondre ensemble." He no longer found God in nature, only the echo of his own sensuality, which demanded the body of another for its satisfaction. However, the ideal shape he projected into the forms of nature was no more than a narcissistic image of himself, the double that he wished to create out of his own being in order to establish a more intimate fusion, to plunge more deeply into a torrential natural unity. Thus confronted with a mere shadow of himself, he finally broke out of his erotic fantasies and objectless desires in the quest of an objective fulfillment. He visited a prostitute.

With the introduction of the prostitute, Marie, Flaubert interrupts the monotone of the narrative voice. Less and less capable of feigning distance on his narrator, he lacks the fictional perspective necessary to sustain the lyricism of a Werther or a René, or the continuity of a *roman intime.* As in the *Mémoires,* he is in fact searching, through thinly veiled autobiography, for such a perspective. Marie represents, therefore, an effort to establish distance and perpetuate the possibility of a fictional narrative.

The narrator describes his experience with Marie in terms of a transcendent sensuality. When he first saw her she was standing against a window, and the light streaming through a yellow curtain illuminated her white gown and dark hair. This image prefigures his perception of her as a madonna of lasciviousness, an all-embracing and caressing mother. Repeating the imagery of his pantheistic ecstasy, he compares her caresses to an ocean, her dress to waves lapping over him, her hair to a sea in which he plunged his head and arms. She completely encircled him, drowning him in the intensity of her gaze: "Ses yeux brillaient, m'enflammaient, son regard m'enveloppait, plus que ses bras, j'étais perdu dans son oeil" (p. 259). Rather than embracing Marie, he was embraced by her, luxuriating not in possession but in being passively absorbed into a presence which seemed more than physical. More than her arms, her eyes—the focus of a passionate recognition—held him. Thus their final embrace, which he describes in the same terms as the union between earth and sea in his pantheistic ecstasy, meant absorption into a compassionate rather than

Novembre: The Failure of the Lyrical Autobiography

an indifferent nature, "a delightful dying."

When he left her, he was overcome by the feeling that his experience had separated him "by an eternity" from what he had been before. As a sensuous ecstasy it had lifted him out of time, but had made him aware, at its end, of the anxiety of falling back into time. Thus, in the fading light, he gazed out of his window: "Le jardin, déjà dans l'ombre, était plein de tristesse, des cercles jaunes et oranges tournaient dans le coin des murs, s'abaissaient et montaient dans les buissons, la terre était sèche et grise" (p. 260).

Throughout *Novembre,* from the first sentence on, we have seen the consistent use of the pathetic fallacy to establish an analogy between human feeling and nature. However, apart from the anthropomorphism of the phrase "le jardin était plein de tristesse," this description of the view from the window marks a new point of departure and prefigures the use of natural imagery in Flaubert's later novels. It is visually detailed, nonanthropomorphic, and nonmetaphorical, while constituting at the same time a highly subjective state of mind. The shadow of the garden, the mobile and revolving circles of light, the dryness and grayness of the earth, can be said to correspond to the narrator's depression, anxiety and sexual depletion, but the term "correspond" suggests a too rigid distinction between object and subject and the inevitable priority of one over the other, the objective description serving, in this case, as a pretext for information about the subject. Unlike his earlier use of the image of the tropical forest to describe the variety of his being, Flaubert's description here is not, properly speaking, symbolic; it is simultaneously both literal and symbolic, both objective and subjective. Significantly, it originated in a moment of separation from the familiar perception of the past, and it embodies the uncanniness of its origin.

However, the narrator moved away from the window, from that brief moment when his familiar self was eclipsed by the image of the garden, and returned to a conscious consideration of a new paradox: he was caught between nauseating satiety and ardent hopes; he desired his desire and missed his vanished joy. He finally overcame this paradox by turning Marie into a synthesis of his earlier fantasies about women and his recently experienced

Novembre: The Failure of the Lyrical Autobiography

sensuality: "Aux imaginations que je m'étais faites naguère que je m'efforçais d'évoquer, se mêlait le souvenir intense de mes dernières sensations, et le tout se confondant, fantôme et corps, rêve et réalité, la femme que je venais de quitter pris pour moi une proportion synthétique; où tout se résuma dans le passé et d'où tout s'élança pour l'avenir" (p. 261). Thus transformed, Marie offered an entirely new point of departure.

Novembre has been characterized thus far by a movement from one extreme to another, from enthusiasm to despair, from spirituality to sensuality, from lyricism to irony, from idealism to materialism. Although this movement has been jerky, full of stops and starts, it has followed a rudimentary dialectical development. Apparent polarities have turned out to be thesis and antithesis, and each new synthesis a new thesis. The transformation of Marie through a synthesis of fantasy and sensuality explicitly names the implicit dialectical structure of the work. Predictably then, returning to the new Marie he had forged in his imagination, the narrator discovered the negative side of her previously positive sensuality.

His second visit took place at night; she was dressed in black. The caressing madonna had turned into an enchantress whose satin robe crackled and sparkled when she moved and whose eyes, no longer the source of ecstasy, compelled him into their malevolent power, and fastened onto him like birds of prey: "Chaque effluve de ce regard béant, semblable aux cercles successifs que décrit l'orfraie, m'attachait de plus en plus à cette magie terrible" (p.261). She had turned into a predator and, imagining he had returned to her out of love, avidly seized upon him as food for her own dreams and desires. Her embrace was that of a wild destructive animal devouring the entrails of its victim: "Et elle appuya sa bouche sur mon cou, y fouillant avec d'âpres baisers, comme une bête fauve au ventre de sa victime" (p. 261). In this context her request for a lock of his hair had sinister implications which come to light indirectly in his general reflections about the meanings of the exchange of hair between lovers. Interrupting his narrative, he muses on the hair of primitive women—which he compares to tufts of palm leaves—and the hair of dead women still clinging to unearthed skulls. Thus, in fantasy, he destroys Marie as she had attempted to destroy him. She had symbolically devoured his flesh and he

63

Novembre: The Failure of the Lyrical Autobiography

symbolically reduces her to bones. His violence is unconscious, however, and, like his imagery, overwrought. Returning to his narrative, he recalls how he scattered faded violets over Marie's satiated and sleeping body, an ambivalent act scarcely distinguishable from a burial.

Hitherto, the narrator has described Marie through the prism of his own distorting emotions: she was a loving force of nature, then the synthesis of fantasy and sensuality, and finally a wild and destructive enchantress. While obviously representing a typical nineteenth-century distortion, this extreme idealization and vilification also represents the narrator's ambivalence about the surrender of his self to sensation. He reasserts himself by distancing himself from Marie, who, in recounting the story of her life, becomes a new narrative voice.

From the beginning, she recalls, she had experienced sensual pleasure as a religious experience. Her first narcissistic ecstasies provoked "cantiques de volupté," and thereafter the sensual high points of her girlhood occurred in religious contexts. In church she stimulated her senses by imagining the naked Christ, enveloped in incense, descending from the cross and moving towards her. Dressed up for her first communion, she gazed enraptured at her image in the mirror, wishing, like the narrator, that her reflection were a real other whom she could embrace. Unlike the narrator, however, she had always thought that indulgence in sensuality was the means to absolute ecstasy.

When she grew up, she sought transcendence through the variety of her lovers—old, young, aristocratic, peasant, monstrous, deformed. However, since what she craved was union with the divine, with an Apollo or a Bacchus, none could satisfy her. Every finite lover was a limitation on her desire for a comprehensive physical satisfaction. She wished to coincide with the very pulse of nature and dreamt of the embrace of serpent or lion. Only when she entered a theater, the focus of all eyes, did she glimpse the satisfaction of being absolutely possessed.

As prostitute, she was able to satisfy both her craving for a variety of physical experiences and a multiplicity of identities. Finally, believing the narrator to be the means to transcendence she had been searching for, she offered herself to him as actress,

Novembre: The Failure of the Lyrical Autobiography

ready to play whatever role he might demand of her—Spanish dancer, savage, painter's model, friend and comrade, assassin's lookout, thief. She had found a lover, she believed, who would satisfy the full range of her repertoire. Indeed, the narrator had longed for such a woman—sensual, passionate, desired by many men, ultimately theatrical—but he discovered that the intensity of her cravings threatened to annihilate him, and he describes their last embrace as a horrendous dance of death in which Marie, a pale and ravenous predator, turned pleasure into delirium and joy into torment.

Marie's autobiography describes in detail the structure of desire, and further elucidates the narrator's own disordered consciousness. She had sought to be entirely possessed but had found her imagination constantly overflowing the material limits of possible sensual gratification. Inevitably in her quest, the "other" could only be an abstract vessel, a thing or a god, existing uniquely for her gratification. Cast in this role, the narrator, who had similarly sought absorption in some divine presence, found himself negated. He in his chastity, she in her sensuality, had followed the same path and had reached the same gulf. Just as Marie is the narrator's mirror image, her narrative voice emerges not as that of an independent fictional character but as the echo of the narrator's own. After all, *he* is telling her story, assuming the first person "I" of her autobiography, and when his identity with Marie becomes apparent, she can no longer survive as an independent reality. Flaubert's attempt to create distance on his narrator through the introduction of Marie ultimately fails.

Although he fled her sensuality, the narrator discovered that her image continued to obsess him as the ideal mediating all other potential objects of desire. Reflecting on this strange occurrence, he recalls a friend "qui avait adoré à quinze ans une jeune mère qu'il avait vue nourrissant son enfant; de longtemps il n'estima que les tailles de poissarde, la beauté des femmes sveltes lui était odieuse" (p. 270)—a thinly disguised reference to Flaubert's first encounter with Elisa Schlésinger who was to become the physical archetype of his fictional heroines. This reference, however, is full of scorn and once again reveals Flaubert's lack of distance on his past. He uses his narrator to desecrate his love for Maria who

Novembre: The Failure of the Lyrical Autobiography

falls from goddess to fishwife.

Transformed by his imagination, Marie became the image of a lost, and never really attained, pleasure, narcissistically binding him to the mirage of a desired fulfillment. Thus, she reemerged as an ideal that he continued to search for in reality. And, obsessed by her image, he would sometimes fantasy, like the madman of the *Mémoires,* that she was present, walking just behind him.

He has described Marie, he informs the reader, in order to make her live again, but he has failed. On the one hand, the picture is incomplete, for he knows more than he has told; on the other, he cannot separate his imagination from the reality and suspects that his memory of her corresponds only to a wish, to a "conception de mon esprit." Was she real, was she imagined? This ambiguity reflects Flaubert's own ambiguity about the status of *Novembre.* Just as the narrator is not sure whether Marie had an independent reality or is merely the creation of his own desires, Flaubert cannot establish whether his narrator is himself or a fictional creation. The narrator's autobiographical "I" is supposed to be that of a fictional character, but it is inseparable from Flaubert's own. And when the former expresses the wish that he could create another being out of thought alone so that he could caress the materialized image of himself, he sums up Flaubert's attitude to *Novembre.* He is still attached to a narcissistic reflection of himself, though he might despair that his reflection does not have any independence.

In this light we can better understand his nostalgia for a language that would establish the analogy—and not the rift—between nature and consciousness. In the course of *Novembre* the narrator becomes increasingly aware that such an analogy is spurious. After he has failed to establish unity with nature either through fantasy or sensation, he finally concludes that while everything is in order in nature, everything is awry in man: "Tout est bien dans la nature, les arbes poussent, les fleuves coulent, les oiseaux chantent, les étoiles brillent; mais l'homme tourmenté remue, s'agite. abat les forêts, bouleverse la terre, s'élance sur la mer, voyage, court, tue les animaux, se tue lui-même et pleure, et rugit, et pense à l'enfer,—comme si Dieu lui avait donné un esprit pour concevoir encore plus de maux qu'il n'endure" (p. 271) Nature

Novembre: The Failure of the Lyrical Autobiography

is complete in itself, but man is incomplete; hence his perpetual agitation. Although he evokes the destruction of nature in terms particularly applicable to the nineteenth century—with its materialism, imperialism, and splenetic frustrations—his use of the imagery of God and Hell suggests something more than a historical aberration. The original malediction is consciousness itself, the ability to imagine more than is experienced. However, in spite of this conclusion, the narrator returns again to a lyrical comparison between himself and nature. Just as the leaf falls and then flies along with the wind, so too would he like to depart, never to return. His autobiography closes on this note of wishful escape as he imagines a variety of exotic journeys.

Whereas, in his description of the discrepancy between man and nature, he had placed the desire for travel in the context both of exploitation of foreign lands and of the malediction of consciousness, he now evokes travel, in the romantic tradition, as the quest for an alternative and fulfilling experience. Thus, after Chateaubriand, he imagines himself in the desert, among savages, in the New World; in India and China, and even (shades of Balzac) in Norway. The impulse underlying this quest is a desire to be part of a more natural society—which lapses into the sentimental nostalgia for the simple life in a Sicilian fishing village and the love of a girl "of the people"—and a desire to exhaust all experience and all the possibilities suggested by the imagination, even if the consequence should be his death. Thus, he recapitulates the two impulses which have hitherto pervaded his autobiography, the impulse towards absorption in a natural immanence and the impulse towards the transcendence of nature and the attainment of an ideal purity. Reflecting a romantic nostalgia for a return to a state of nature and anticipating a symbolist leap "anywhere out of this world," he cannot immediately find, either in life or art, any fulfillment.

Although at this point the narrator puts down his pen, this is not the last we hear of him or his life. A second narrator introduces himself to complete the story of "his friend." On the surface this narrative device seems to resemble the literary genre common in the eighteenth and early nineteenth centuries, in which the author masquerades as the editor of a manuscript which

Novembre: The Failure of the Lyrical Autobiography

he has come upon by chance or which was left to him by some luckless friend. In the eighteenth century the genre aimed at convincing the reader of the truth of the material presented, most often a collection of letters, and in many cases, as with *La Vie de Marianne* and *La Nouvelle Héloïse,* many readers did believe that they were reading authentic and not invented documents. With the advent of romanticism, the pseudoeditor abandoned the collection of letters for fictional autobiography and, putting the fictional "I" in parenthesis, as it were, called upon the reader to accept the authenticity of the material but to question the authenticity of the autobiographer. By definition, the author disclaimed identity with the hero of his novel and took an a priori distance on the pathos or moral ambiguities of a Werther or an Adolphe. Although *Novembre* follows the tradition of the romantic autobiography, the introduction of the second narrator is very much at odds with the traditional use of the pseudoeditor.

Flaubert lacks the traditional distance on his narrator and is so intricately bound up with him that he shares all his confusions about his past and all his uncertainty about his future. He finds it difficult at times to continue writing because he has no preconceived plan in mind and cannot see any outcome—hence the constant false starts and renewed beginnings. He attempts in the process of writing to create that distance on his narrator, as with the episode of Marie, which would enable him to assume the perspective which should have been his point of departure. The introduction of the second narrator is not therefore an organic prerequisite to the work, but something of an afterthought. In fact, Flaubert added this last section of *Novembre* some eight months after abandoning the work in order to complete a text which, like the original narrator himself, hung precariously in mid-air.

In *L'Idiot de la famille* Sartre explains this transition from first to second narrator as a consequence of Flaubert's failures in Paris—both in his law studies and in his social ambitions—which forced him to look with a demystifying eye on his former pretentions and illusions of grandeur. In Sartre's view, the introduction of the second narrator permits Flaubert to assume the persona of the objective observer and to reject, with an irritated superiority, the subjective meanderings of his former self. At the same time

Novembre: The Failure of the Lyrical Autobiography

it permits him to justify the work (which he very much enjoyed reading to friends such as Maxime Du Camp, Louise Colet, and the Goncourt brothers) as the authentic document of a deluded state of mind. However, Sartre goes on, it also means that Flaubert splits himself in two and objectifies and "derealizes" himself as his own family had objectified and derealized him. Thus, the second narrator becomes a doctor or a policeman carrying on an investigation into the physical and social pathology of the first, and the scene is set for the literal splitting of the psyche which shattered Flaubert in his first nervous crisis, some fourteen months after he had finished *Novembre*. At the same time Sartre identifies this splitting of the self as the rejection of the "mirage of subjectivity" and the emergence of the perspective of the novelist: "The actor asks: What is there behind my roles? What makes me play these roles—always the same ones—rather than others? To put the imaginary into question is to look behind permanent derealization for the reality which reveals and directs it. Behind the 'eagle flights,' Flaubert, disabused, wishes to discover 'the small true fact.' "[6] While the introduction of the second narrator certainly permitted Flaubert to find an ending for *Novembre,* is it true, as Sartre maintains, that the second narrator objectifies the first and, if it exists, does this objectification mean a pathological splitting of the psyche or—and Sartre confusingly identifies the two processes—the emergence of the objective novelist?

The second narrator certainly seems to separate himself from the first, pitying the reader for having had to tolerate such boring puerilities in such a metaphorical, hyperbolic, and generally highfalutin style. Moreover, he claims that he has had no connection with the previous narrator since he lapsed into silence except, of course, for his manuscript: "Ni dans sa conversation, ni dans ses lettres, ni dans les papiers que j'ai fouillés après sa mort, et où ceci se trouvait, je n'ai saisi rien qui dévoilât l'état de son âme, à partir de l'époque òu il cessa d'écrire ses confessions" (p. 274). However, both of these stances, which fall within the traditional pseudoeditorial framework, are completely belied by his subsequent transparent approval and intimate knowledge of the first narrator's state of mind, even though, as he maintains, he had had no verbal or written communication with him.

Novembre: The Failure of the Lyrical Autobiography

After abandoning his manuscript the first narrator left the provinces for Paris, where his loneliness was exacerbated by the presence of the bourgeoisie and his love of beauty thwarted by a pervasive ugliness which, in his estimation, amounted to a crime. Immediately the second narrator expresses his sympathy for his friend's reactions and in a typical aside elaborates on them: "C'est en effet quelque chose d'atroce qu'un être laid, de loin il épouvante, de près il dégoûte; quand il parle on souffre; s'il pleure ses larmes vous agacent" (p. 274). And in spite of criticism (which, in the context, really amounts to flattery) of his excesses, he acknowledges that the latter showed good sense in not taking the legal profession seriously, that his good taste prevented him from being a critic, that he was too much the poet to succeed in letters, and that the very idea of having to "assume a position," the constant maxim on the lips of the bourgeois, was barely comprehensible. Furthermore, he advocates withdrawal from the reality of Parisian life and from action in the world, and substantiates that the imagination alone can offer any satisfaction. This endorsement of the first narrator by the second hardly seems to reflect, as Sartre suggests, a demystification of earlier ambition or delusion. On the contrary, it reinforces many of the attitudes in *Novembre* which Flaubert, through his many stops and starts, had put into question. The "mirage of subjectivity" is in fact more alive than ever.

Nor is the second narrator's frequently scathing irony proof of a new, "objective" point of departure. It merely accentuates and continues the irony which constantly broke through the lyrical voice of the previous narrator. It signifies neither novelistic impersonality nor detachment but is a correlative to the grandiose "eagle flights" in that it affirms the superiority of the ironist over the mass of men whom he perceives as brutal, greedy, and deformed.

The sympathetic identification of the second narrator with the first reaches its high point in the description of the latter's return, motivated by nervous irritation and loneliness, to the scene of his greatest ecstasy, the pantheistic vision he had had on the way to X.[7] Everything had changed. It was winter; the ditches were filled with ice, the trees bare, the sky leaden. Even the posts which

Novembre: The Failure of the Lyrical Autobiography

had indicated the way were overturned. What had once been a yielding organic presence had frozen into an unyielding metallic mass. The leaves, which had once meant lightness and the natural movement of memory, formed a hard, black layer on the ground. In the village of X itself the quay was deserted, people had locked themselves in their houses, icicles hung from the roofs, and the creaking of the shop signs echoed the chainlike sound of the ocean as it came up over the rocks. The first narrator's reaction (which is fully interiorized by the second narrator) to this change was an indulgent self-pity, embodied in his affectionate identification with the stranded "corpse" of an old boat, half-buried under the sand and encrusted with mussels and polyps, and in his likening of the falling snowflakes to "huge silver tears."

Thus the narrator (in this passage it is impossible to separate the second from the first) no longer found in nature an all-embracing presence but still identified with it by means of the pathetic fallacy. Winter reflected back the image of his state of mind just as, at the beginning of *Novembre,* autumn had signified the mellowness of remembering. There was still, therefore, no real separation between himself and nature. However, in the following description of nightfall, which is the polar opposite of his pantheistic ecstasy, a real separation occurs.

Crouching in a hollow made by hunters—the antithesis of the pastoral furrow which had been his previous vantage point: "il vit un instant l'image de la lune rouler sur les flots et remuer dans la mer comme un grand serpent, puis de tous les côtés du ciel, des nuages s'amoncelèrent de nouveau, et tout fut noir. Dans les ténèbres, les flots ténébreux se balançaient, montaient les uns sur les autres et détonnaient comme cent canons, une sorte de rythme faisait de ce bruit une mélodie terrible, le rivage, vibrant sous le coup des vagues, répondait à la haute mer retentissante" (p. 276). In this description nature can hardly be grasped as a concrete presence. We are aware only of the *image* of the moon moving over the waves; the gathering clouds disappear into blackness; it is virtually impossible to visualize the dark waves against the general background of darkness, and their movement culminates in a metaphor that appeals to the ear rather than the eye. We move far away from the literal, concrete presence of nature by means

Novembre: The Failure of the Lyrical Autobiography

of the metaphors of the snake and the hundred resounding cannons—both of which are sinister, the snake traditionally connoting a fall from natural harmony, the cannons connoting destruction and conflict. However, both of these describe an *aesthetic* experience, the first the patterning of the moon's shadow on the sea, and the second a terrible melody. Like the image of the setting sun at the close of the *Mémoires,* these images evoke the coming into being of the imaginative consciousness. Significantly, the persona of the crouching and silent observer is eclipsed. Nature, as described here, offers no foothold, only image upon receding image, a temporality which can neither be transcended nor negated.

At this point the passage comes to an abrupt end and the second narrator reemerges to sum up the destiny of the first. After this experience, we are told, the first narrator contemplated suicide, then drifted back to Paris which, in a typical reversal, briefly assumed a positive aspect, and finally lapsed into death through sheer mental attrition, "par la seule force de la pensée."

Thus, having momentarily transcended the self-pity and reifying irony of his two narrators, Flaubert assumes once again the cynical persona of the second narrator and detaches himself from the first. Those who have genuinely suffered, he writes, will find it difficult to believe in such a strange way of dying, but they should tolerate it "for love of the marvellous," and because it appears in a novel. With this interruption he not only denies the sympathetic identification with the first narrator which has hitherto characterized his narrative, but, more surprisingly, he shatters the illusion that he is an editor presenting an authentic document to the public and merely rounding out a factual account of events. He tears off the mask and admits that he is the author of a novel. And his implied definition of "novel" is pejorative: it deals in fiction, not the fiction that embodies a more fundamental truth than fact but the fiction which fraudulently lies. Thus, he not only calls attention to the artificiality of his protagonist's death, but in suggesting that real suffering does not lead to such an extravagant death, he questions his emotional authenticity. What is the meaning of this abrupt reversal and what, to reraise Sartre's question, is Flaubert's relation to his two narrators?

Novembre: The Failure of the Lyrical Autobiography

This criticism by the second narrator of the possible inauthenticity of the first does not mark a new development. As we have seen at the beginning of his narrative, the former has already criticized the falseness and hyperbole apparent in the language of the document that had, by chance, fallen into his possession. Moreover, in his autobiography the first narrator frequently addresses such criticism to himself: at one moment he indulgently displays the subtleties of his suffering sensibility, while at the next he bitterly denounces his emotional shallowness and lack of a passionate center, his derivative imitations of romantic heroes and romantic writers. However, does this alternation between extravagant self-praise and indulgent self-criticism become, as Sartre suggests, a schizophrenic doubling when the first person of the original narrator splits into two with the introduction of the second narrator when the confused "I" becomes a detached "I" describing another part of the self as "he"?

The main problem with such an interpretation is that the "detachment" of the second narrator, whom Sartre compares to a doctor or policeman, is extremely dubious. In fact, far from reifying and derealizing his "other self," he most often justifies and defends him as a martyr of both the imagination and the bourgeoisie. His assumption of the third-person point of view is only a logical expression of the pseudodistance of the emotion of self-pity which underlies the shifting and indeterminate perspectives of the autobiographical section of *Novembre.* He is neither doctor nor censor but a barely veiled Narcissus.

This is not to deny, of course, that Flaubert continues in *Novembre* the portrayal of radical alienation already begun in the *Mémoires.* In the *Mémoires* he explicitly admits that his narrative "I" has no center or continuity of being, and the madness he describes assumes an intensity that leads to physical vertigo and the most terrifying schizophrenic dreams. In *Novembre* his narrator's alienation from reality, his extreme fluctuations between delusions of omnipotence and catatonic depressions, lead to actual fits and even death. But in both works the act of writing establishes a minimal distance on the narrative persona, and *this* distance is neither that which splits the self into two pathological and unsynthesized elements nor that of the truly objective and untendentious

Novembre: The Failure of the Lyrical Autobiography

novelist.

In *Novembre* Flaubert remains narcissistically and self-pityingly attached to his alienated persona, yet in the course of writing he dialectically explores the limits of his alienation and effects syntheses which prefigure, in a rudimentary way, his later novelistic points of view. He has not yet become an "objective" novelist —which will not mean, as Sartre implies, the reification of the self but the synthesis of the varied reified elements of the self. However, like the introduction of the voice of Marie, the transition to the second narrator attempts to mediate the antithetical but equally solipsistic tendencies towards an ideal flight into fantasy and a cynical exposure of the power of materiality. It does not entirely succeed, and the second narrator, like Marie, merely holds up a mirror to the distortions of his predecessor. He neither transcends nor demystifies them. At the end of *Novembre* Flaubert acknowledges his failure to resolve his two selves when he questions the emotional authenticity of the first narrator and reveals that the truth originally claimed by the second is only a contrived and artificial fiction. He had initially attempted to create unity through the lyrical identification between mind and nature, but, as he wrote, this identification became more and more tenuous until, with the return to X, it collapsed completely. The return to X brings to a climax the perception, continually glimpsed and evaded throughout the work, that the creative standpoint embodies a consciousness of death, of a temporality distinct from the nontime of eternal Idea or Matter. Flaubert flees such a perception but, in acknowledging the flight, keeps the possiblity alive of a new point of departure.

NOTES

1. Jean Bruneau, *Les Débuts littéraires de Gustave Flaubert* (Paris, 1962), p. 335 (translation).
2. Flaubert's use of language here prefigures Baudelaire's *Spleen.* It evokes in particular the opening line: "J'ai plus de souvenirs que si j'avais mille ans."

Novembre: The Failure of the Lyrical Autobiography

3. In the *Mémoires* Flaubert also uses the carriage as the scene for the overwhelming sense of vertigo which struck him when he left Marie. It is an appropriate figure (which reaches its fullest elaboration in *Madame Bovary*) to describe the alienation between the isolated self and a reality perceived merely as images passing consecutively by. The uncanny thing is that Flaubert's first and, for his literary career, decisive nervous attack will actually take place, some fourteen months after he has finished *Novembre,* in a carriage.
4. This description exactly prefigures Flaubert's first nervous collapse on the way to Pont-l'Eveque. It vividly shows that he had a keen vision of the intentionality and structure of his psyche.
5. This passage suggests an interesting refutation of René Girard's *Mensonge romantique et vérité romanesque* (Paris, 1961). Like Girard, Flaubert sees the dangers of the solipsistic and self-divinizing romantic imagination, but unlike him, he does not posit only two kinds of mediation between man and the world, that is, Christ or one's neighbor; language—if it is both subjective and objective, neither autonomous nor imitative but truly ambivalent—also offers a real, and perhaps the only mediation.
6. Sartre, *L'Idiot de la famille,* 2.1725.
7. The origin of this *topos* of the return can be traced to J.-J. Rousseau's *La Nouvelle Héloise,* to Saint-Preux's return to Meillerie, the scene of the most significant experience of his past. An extended comparison of the function of the *topos* in the two works would reveal the radical differences between Rousseau and the young Flaubert. In brief, the return to Meillerie, the *reflection* of the previous experience, is emblemized by sun and an atmosphere of *bonheur,* whereas the original experience was characterized by suffering and appropriately harsh weather. Rousseau accepts the sacrifice of the original experience as a genuine sacrifice; Flaubert refuses, in this context, to make such a sacrifice.

4

L'Éducation sentimentale (of 1845): Jules' Aesthetic Conversion

Flaubert began the first *Éducation* in February 1843 and completed it, after long periods of inactivity, in January 1845. This period was of critical importance in his life and aesthetic development. In January of 1844 he experienced a devastating nervous seizure. It occurred while he was driving in a cabriolet with his brother Achille, toward Deauville. They had just left Pont-l'Évêque; it was pitch black when a carter's wagon approached them from the opposite direction. Flaubert suddenly let go of the reins and fell to the floor as if dead. He finally came to himself in a neighboring house where his brother had taken him. He later recalled that he had experienced the sudden explosion of lights, like a massive fireworks display. This attack, which was to recur in an attenuated form over the next years, and which always incorporated the details of the first episode, effected a change not only upon his career—henceforth the law was out of the question—but upon his conception of himself. In a letter to Louise Colet (27 August 1846) he wrote the following about this event: "J'ai eu deux existences bien distinctes; les évènements extérieurs ont été le symbole de la fin de la première et de la naissance de la seconde; tout cela est mathématique. Ma vie active, passionnée, émue, pleine de soubresauts opposés et de sensations multiples, a fini à vingt-deux ans. A cette époque, j'ai fait de grands progrès tout à coup; et autre chose est venue."

L'Éducation sentimentale: Jules' Aesthetic Conversion

This attack occurred during the composition of the *Éducation.* Although there is no specific reference to the episode, Jules, frustrated in both his literary and sentimental aspirations, the surrogate of Flaubert himself, undergoes what can only be called a conversion, leading to a radical redefinition of his relationship to life and literature. This conversion changes the entire direction of the *Éducation,* finally sabotaging its original aesthetic intent. It is therefore tempting to read into this conversion Flaubert's own new point of departure, an act of aesthetic faith in the future which, precisely on account of its visionary self-evidence, seems to bear the stamp of truth.

Originally the hero of the *Éducation* was not Jules but Henry, a young man from the provinces who goes to Paris, has a passionate love affair with a married woman, runs away with her to America where the passion disintegrates under the pressures of poverty and habit, and finally returns to France where he successfully affiliates himself to bourgeois society. Henry represents Flaubert's alter ego, the successful accomplishment of an integration within society of which the latter's studies in the law were a necessary debut. However, being "other" to his main character, Flaubert could not help creating his own counterpoint to Henry in the character of Jules, whom he himself calls a "repoussoir." Although there is little initial difference between the two characters—both are from the provinces, suffer from an excess of sensibility, and have a great love of literature—Jules as reflective writer is already an implicit negation of the more worldly Henry, who leaves the provinces for Paris. Flaubert's condescending irony towards Henry is apparent in the first sentence of the novel: "Le héros de ce livre, un matin d'octobre, arriva à Paris avec un coeur de dix-huit ans et un diplôme de bachelier ès lettres."

In creating Jules as the implicit negation of Henry, Flaubert returns once again to the double perspective that characterizes both the *Mémoires* and *Novembre.* But this double perspective no longer emanates from a single divided personality; rather, it is an extension of the pseudo third person of the last pages of *Novembre* into two separate fictional identities. The structure of the *Éducation* therefore possesses an inherent doubleness. Flaubert devotes alternating sections to Jules and Henry in which each has the dom-

L'Éducation sentimentale: Jules' Aesthetic Conversion

inating focus. We have the impression of reading two novels in one. This lack of integration is reflected in Flaubert's perspective as novelist. He constantly intrudes in the novel, making observations on his characters' actions and adding his own moral digressions.

While Henry habituates himself to Paris, Jules lives a basically static existence sustained only by the hope that his play will be performed by Bernardi, the manager of a travelling troupe of players, and that his love for Lucinde, an actress in the company, will be returned. He lives in the hope of a potential fulfillment while he is forced to take a demeaning post as a clerk in which he foresees the horrible parody of an authentic act of creation: "Donc, j'aurai un maître, un supérieur, un chef, à qui il faudra obéir, à qui j'irai porter la besogne, l'ouvrage, et qui sera là, assis dans son fauteuil, à examiner tout, à compter les virgules passées, les lignes de travers, les mots oubliés, et qui me grondera sur ma mauvaise lecture et me bousculera comme un valet" (p. 280). We perceive Jules mostly through the letters he writes to Henry, who is engaged in life like the conventional fictional hero of a novel. Jules therefore maintains a basically autobiographical perspective which almost by definition is the expression of a division within himself. Flaubert writes of him: "Ce qui le rendait à plaindre, c'est qu'il ne savait pas bien distinguer ce qui est de ce qui devrait être; il souffrait toujours de quelque chose qui lui manquait, il attendait sans cesse je ne sais quoi qui n'arrivait jamais" (p. 308). Henry était plus libre, plus léger, plus net dans ses allures; Jules qu'il y eut entre Henry et lui, c'étaient deux hommes fort distincts: Henry, on the other hand, possesses unity: "Quelque ressemblance était toujours gêné comme quelqu'un qui étouffe, il était plus exagéré, plus entêté, plus absurde; seulement il y avait une disproportion naturelle à rire de lui-même, quand il se regardait à froid, qui était bien loin de la chaleureuse tenacité d'Henry. . . ." (p. 308)

With a rather heavy-handed irony Flaubert reveals the divergence between the two characters mostly by the contrast between Jules' letters lamenting his constant disappointments and the successful destiny of Henry. This irony reaches its climax when Henry, who has just written a letter to Jules describing his successful seduction of Mme Renaud, receives a letter from Jules describing

L'Éducation sentimentale: Jules' Aesthetic Conversion

Lucinde's betrayal and departure. This in fact marks the turning point of the novel, the point at which Jules and Henry begin their separate and irreconcilable existences.

Jules' description of the departure of the acting troupe is the description of a profound crisis which, whether it was written before or after Flaubert's crisis at Pont-l'Évêque—and one must take into account Flaubert's uncannily prefigurative imagination—puts an end, as did Flaubert's crisis, to a phase of his existence. Finding Lucinde's hotel room empty, except for a few curl papers and hairpins, Jules discovers that not only has she left with the troupe but that they have left him their bills to pay. He rushes after them along the deserted Paris road bordered by its rows of poplars and swept with a glacial wind and swirling dust. When he reaches the next village, where he hopes to find them, he blacks out: "Je ne me rappelle plus rien. Il y avait seulement, sur un vieux pont, un moulin qui m'eclaboussa en passant; après le pont la côte commençait. La rage me redonna des forces et je voulus la monter, mais, n'en pouvant plus, je tombai à un détour sur le bord de la route, la mort dans l'âme, râlant, brisé" (p. 313).

Raising his head, he perceives a black spot on the highway growing smaller and smaller and a faint rumbling sound. From time to time the distant coach stops. Then, suddenly, in the brilliant light of the sun, he makes out the figure of Bernardi offering his arm to Lucinde. This telescopic sight is visionary: "Et puis, tous les objets grandirent et je les vis nettement. Bernardi donnait le bras à Lucinde, il s'approcha d'elle et l'embrassa, je crois qu'ils riaient et qu'ils parlaient de moi" (p. 313). As the coach departs again, he presses his ear to the ground to catch the echoes of its rumblings. He returns to the bridge and finds himself beckoned by the waters below, but he is approached by a little girl in rags who smiles at him as she begs for charity. Overcome by a desire to destroy her along with himself, he screams at her to go away. The rest of the day he wanders sadly, like a wolf, through the countryside, in a state of madness, bleeding from the brambles he has inadvertently brushed against. Finally, as darkness falls, he follows a wagoner to his farm: ". . . mes tempes bourdonnaient, et je ne savais où aller, la misère me tenait, j'avais froid, j'avais faim, je grelottais, j'avais peur de tout" (p. 313). At the farm he is fed

L'Éducation sentimentale: Jules' Aesthetic Conversion

bread and milk and slowly comes to himself again.

There are uncanny parallels between this crisis and Flaubert's crisis at Pont-l'Évêque. Jules loses his senses on a highway, he is obsessed by the rumbling of the coach, he perceives details of the scene in a visionary way, he feels he is dying and longs to die and, finally, he comes to himself in a nearby farm. This loss of self has already been prefigured in the *Mémoires* when Flaubert, returning in a cabriolet from the scene where he had met Maria (Elisa), experienced his past as a swirling chaos. Moreover, Jules' desire to drown himself picks up not only a detail from *Novembre* but the nightmare of the drowning mother from the *Mémoires* which left the narrator filled with the same rage and despair. Thus, this crisis not only appears to refer to Flaubert's major crisis, but subsumes the crises of his earlier works.

The experience leaves Jules only half alive, with a broken will. As he writes to Henry: "... je vais et je vis comme une roue qu'on a poussé et qui roulera jusqu'à ce qu'elle tombe... chose inerte qui se trouve là sans cause, créée par une force incompréhensible et qui ne comprend rien à elle-même" (p. 313). He then passes into a state of "désespoir réfléchi." Although he makes an effort to analyze and relive his past, even visiting the places where he had encountered Lucinde, it remains dreamlike: "... les événements passés lui faisaient l'effet d'un de ces rêves sans nom, où l'on a vu des beautés surhumaines et des supplices inouïs, et dont le souvenir vague est un supplice" (p. 320). (This recollection seems to refer to Flaubert's crisis rather than to Jules' past with Lucinde.) This voluntary effort leaves him only with a gallery of unconnected pictures. Denigrating both love and poetry, he lives the banal routine of a convalescent, not participating in life, which he perceives as a meaningless masked ball. Thus, he lives in a kind of death, buried, as he says, in his sloth like a marmot under the snow.

Jules' inauthenticity reaches a climax at the very moment Henry is experiencing the decadence of his love affair with Mme Renaud. Faced with the real pressures of his poverty in America and his real disillusion with his mistress, Henry immediately recognizes the falseness and self-indulgence of Jules' letters: "...c'était une série de plaintes et de doléances delayée dans un style travaillé,

L'Éducation sentimentale: Jules' Aesthetic Conversion

farci de métaphores incongrues; le ton général était amer et guindé, l'ironie intentionnelle, forcée, tandis que les endroits langoureux—il y en avait quelques uns—décelaient une sensibilité puérile et maladive" (p. 344). Through this alien persona Flaubert demystifies the self-indulgence of Jules as he did that of the narrators of the *Mémoires* and *Novembre*. Jules' self-analysis is false since it is based on a desire for self-degradation: ". . . il se détaillait, se décrivait, s'analysait, jusqu'à la dernière fibre, se regardait au microscope ou se regardait dans son ensemble; on eut dit que son orgeuil l'avait placé au-dessus de lui-même et qu'il se voyait avec pitié" (p. 345).

But just as Henry returns to France and begins his conversion into a bourgeois, Jules also experiences the conversion which will turn him into an artist—or so at least Flaubert would have us believe. However, the chapter (26) which describes the conversion is introduced in a rather ambiguous way. Flaubert describes Jules' epochal experience as "lamentable": "À peu près dans ce temps-là, il arriva à Jules une chose lamentable. . . ." Jules is walking in the fields on a calm autumn evening. As in the ecstatic moments of the *Mémoires* and *Novembre,* all is silent but for the rhythm of his walking. In this serene moment he recalls all the experiences he has had in this same countryside which seems to *resume* his past: "Tous ces arbres avaient reçu ses regards, soit sereins et purs, soit sombres et voilés de larmes; il avait erré dans tous ces chemins, radieux et dans la plénitude de sa force, ainsi que la poitrine serrée par le chagrin et l'ennui l'enveloppant dans la tourmente" (p. 350). In spite of comparing his "jours évanouis" to faces in a crowd, "plus divers entre eux que les visages de la foule quand on la regarde passer," he finds their reflection in the landscape before him and admires in himself a certain serene immobility; "Il admirait dans son âme cette grandeur douce et pacifique." However, the voice of Flaubert enters, strangely shattering this pantheistic vision reminiscent of *Novembre*: "Les fleurs croissent dans les fentes des vieux murs; plus la ruine est ancienne, plus elles la couvrent; mais il n'en est point au milieu des ruines du coeur de l'homme, le printemps ne fleurit pas sur ses débris. Les champs de bataille reverdissent, les coquelicots et les roses poussent autour des tombeaux qui finissent par se cacher sous la terre

81

L'Éducation sentimentale: Jules' Aesthetic Conversion

et par s'y ensevelir à leur tour; la pensée n'a pas ce privilege, elle contemple elle-même son éternité et s'en effraye, comme un roi lié sur son trône et qui ne pourrait fuir" (p. 350). In this comparison between natural and human time, Jules reveals his own reified attitude to his past. Although he perceives the anxiety of thought contemplating itself, the comparison he makes between thought and a king tied to his throne expresses his own refusal of thought, his desire to stand above it and at the same time flee it. As his past reemerges, he is afraid of the fidelity of his memories, "rendus plus vivaces encore par la présence de ces lieux où ils avaient été des faits et des sentiments," and wonders if they all belonged to the same man, if a single life was sufficient to embrace them, and he attempts to tie them to some other lost existence, "tant son passé était loin de lui" (p. 350). He looks at his past with astonishment, incapable of perceiving the motives of his emotions or the transitions between them. But at the same time he recognizes that his dissociation is an expression of his emotional deadness, an apparent calm which was in reality a vicious circle: "Tout en irritant sa sensibilité par son imagination, il tâchait que son esprit en annulât les effets, et que le sérieux de la sensation s'en allât rapide comme elle" (p. 350).

He rejects the arid, ironic heights he had sought as a product of his pride and of his refusal of feeling: "Injuste pour son passé, dur pour lui-même, dans ce stoicisme surhumain il en était venu à oublier ses propres passions et à ne plus bien comprendre celle qu'il avait eues; s'il ne s'était pas senti chaque jour forcé, comme artiste, de les étudier et de les rechercher chez les autres, puis de les reproduire par la forme la plus concrète et la plus saillante, ou de les admirer sous la plastique du style, je crois qu'il les eut presque méprisées et il en serait arrivé à cet excès d'inintelligence" (p. 350). It is with some surprise, then, that he finds his past spontaneously come to his mind, from his earliest memories of love to the humiliation of his falls. And instead of feeling a void between himself and his past, he sees himself as its unifying locus, that present state which is the result and sum of his preceding states. However, despite this language of simple cause and effect, Jules' description of his relationship to his past contains certain complexities: "Il avait tiré, par exemple, des théories de la volupté

L'Éducation sentimentale: Jules' Aesthetic Conversion

qu'il ne sentait plus, et la sienne était arrivé enfin comme la conclusion des faits; si elle était fausse, c'est qu'elle était incomplète; si elle était étroite, il fallait tâcher de l'élargir. Il y avait donc une conséquence et une suite dans cette série de perceptions diverses, c'était un problème dont chaque degré pour le résoudre est une solution partielle" (p. 351). In perceiving that every consequence is only another step in the solution of a problem, he describes an endless process and admits that the last word in such a process never arrives. He thus reenvisages his relationship to his past not through the spatial metaphor of a king on his throne, in which the past is in one place and himself in another, but as a temporal process of which he is the essential articulation in the movement from sensation to thought, and, on a more inclusive level, from thought to sensation, ad infinitum. But since there is no point in waiting for the last word, he wonders whether art might not be a way of anticipating it. He then conceives of an art in which he might synthesize his past by means of absolute principles, namely, the principles of natural harmony. As artist, he would step outside the circle of his passions: ". . . Quiconque est engagé dans l'action n'en voit pas l'ensemble." Art will reflect nature, which in turn reflects the face of God. Clearly, this theory of art is in conflict with Jules' earlier perception that his past cannot be reduced to absolute principles since he is constantly in process and must constantly reinterpret it. Just as he previously dissociated himself from his past, he now wishes to stand outside the work. Art will not be an act of creation, or even of interpretation, but will reproduce an already existent harmony. Contemplating the prospect of such an art, he is so uplifted that he loses all sense of where he is and what he has been thinking: "Où était-il donc? dans quel lieu? à quelle heure du jour? qu'avait-il fait? qu'avait-il pensé? Il cherchait à se rattrapper lui-même et à rentrer dans la réalité d'où il était sorti" (p. 351). At this moment a strange dog appears.

The dog rushes at him and licks his hands, yelping and sobbing. It is thin and as narrow as a wolf, wild and wretched. Limping, it fixes its eyes on Jules and turns around him. Jules is struck with horror and then pity for this animal who no longer has any master, who has obviously been maltreated, the kind of dog one finds dead on the side of a highway. But as the animal persists,

L'Éducation sentimentale: Jules' Aesthetic Conversion

he throws a stone at it to go away, which it refuses to do. At this point Jules wonders whether he has not seen this dog before, whether it might not be Fox, the pet spaniel he gave to Lucinde. Full of compassion for this "être inférieur," he recalls the past when he used to play with Fox, in his mistress's presence. But he is repelled once again by the strange dog when he strokes it and discovers not Fox's silky coat but a rough, raw skin. The dog continues to follow him, and in spite of his disgust and horror Jules cannot help being fascinated by it: "Mais aussitôt une voix secrète, puissante, l'appelait vers le monstre, y il y revenait malgré lui" (p. 352). Making a last effort to rid himself of what he calls "cette illusion," he approaches the dog menacingly, whereupon the latter howls but still looks at him tenderly.

Jules continues to walk and the dog continues to follow him, until, just before they reach the river bridge, the dog goes ahead of him and in a strange state of nervousness and rage keeps returning to a certain spot under the arch of the bridge, as if signalling something. Jules attempts to decipher the dog's strange movements and sounds, but they remain a mystery to him: ". . . et il imporait au hasard une puissance inattendue, qui puisse le mettre en rapport avec les secrets révélés par cette voix et l'initier à ce langage, plus muet pour lui qu'une porte fermée" (p. 353). And then he suddenly remembers that it was from this bridge that he had wanted to drown himself. What was there hidden in the river that the dog should so persistently return to it? He imagines it must be Lucinde and then, in a vision, actually sees Lucinde in a white dress, borne along, like Ophelia, on the water. As the moon comes up, two flames appear to pass from the dog's eyes to those of Jules, and there is a growing and seductive sympathetic fusion between the beast and the man, who finds himself mirrored in the dog's eyes. But the fascination turns to fear, and Jules finally wishes it dead as he kicks it in the face. The dog persists, however, in following him back to the town. It seems impervious to blows, capable of sudden disappearance and reappearance, hardly material at all. Sometimes Jules hears its steps behind him, but when he turns around there is nothing there: "Une fois cependant il entendit nettement ses pas, il les reconnut; alors, sans regarder en arrière, il donna un grand coup de pied dans le vide" (p. 353).

L'Éducation sentimentale: Jules' Aesthetic Conversion

When he gets to his house, he bolts the door and goes to his room to reflect upon the strange occurrence. He tries to find the cause of what happened, is sure that he did not simply dream it —which makes him doubt the reality of life: ". . . il y avait quelque chose de si intime, de si net en même temps, qu'il fallait bien reconnaître une réalité d'une autre espèce et aussi réelle que le vulgaire, cependant, tout en semblant le contredire. Or, ce que l'existence offre de tangible, de sensible, disparaissait à sa pensée, comme secondaire et inutile, et comme une illusion qui n'est que la superficie" (p. 354). As if wagering on the truth of this insight, he goes down to the street to see if the dog has indeed followed him. As he hoped and thought, he finds it sitting on the doorstep. Thus, the chapter which Flaubert had introduced as a lamentable episode in Jules' life closes, and the next begins: "Or ce fut son dernier jour de pathétique; depuis, il se corrigea de ses peurs superstitieuses et ne s'effraya pas de rencontrer des chiens galeux dans la campagne." And the rest of the novel is devoted to Jules' corrections of his erroneous conception of literature and the elaboration of a new aesthetics.

As Demorest in his *L'Oeuvre de Gustave Flaubert* has pointed out, the episode of the dog embarrasses the reader. It is badly prepared, and it is difficult to grasp its connection to what follows. Yet the majority of critics have interpreted it as the authentic turning point in the book rather than asking why it is so awkward and unconvincing. It is taken as Flaubert's rejection of the grotesque in literature, the acceptance of the past as the condition of recovery from it, the transition between mysticism and realism, the recognition that personal suffering forms the basis of artistic creation.[1] Jean Bruneau interprets Jules' rejection of the dog as a relapse into false consciousness, "a last attack of the sickness from which Jules has so long suffered"—the refusal of reality.[2] He interprets Jules' final acceptance of the dog as Flaubert's recognition that there are no privileged experiences and that everything in mind and nature is harmoniously regulated by the same laws. Previously his pantheistic vision had been limited to the private ecstasy arising from the contemplation of natural phenomena; now, through Jules, he supposedly grasps it in general, impersonal terms: "Jules is wrong in refusing reality, in being afraid of it, in

85

L'Éducation sentimentale: Jules' Aesthetic Conversion

relating it too directly to himself, to his past, in not seeing its impersonal character and its infinite greatness."³ Jules' acceptance of the dog is thus a reaffirmation of the aesthetics he had formulated before the encounter, of the law of unity existing in the natural world. Sartre suggests that the episode is a *symbolic* description of Flaubert's crisis at Pont-l'Évêque, in which the dog represents a totalization of the past which Jules/Flaubert escapes by sequestration: "The dog is the temptation towards pathos; at the same time it is his past life, his loves, his disappointments, Lucinde, the desperate hours when he contemplates suicide, a few instants of illusory happiness. . . . let us say that this brusk encounter with life corresponds to his crisis (it is his last day of pathos)."⁴ Sartre's interpretation of the encounter with the dog as a "cover event" which reveals and masks at the same time the real event of Pont-l'Évêque has the advantage of attempting to account for its apparent superficiality. But he interprets the surreality of the encounter, in which reality in its more banal manifestations breaks down, as the equivalent of a religious or metaphysical conversion from which Jules' subsequent aesthetics naturally flows.

Let us look again at the context in which the dog appears. Jules has spontaneously overcome his dissociation from the past that began with Lucinde's betrayal. He fully accepts every phase of his past as inseparable from his present. Moreover, he perceives that he is the constant interpreter of his experience, creating synthesis and new thesis and antithesis. His choice of art as the way of "having the last word" does not logically follow from the preceding; it is the expression of a wish, a wish to believe in a pantheism which would not only be a guarantee of harmony but which would establish an equal harmony between microcosm, and macrocosm, namely, between himself and nature. Once again he finds a way of rejecting his past in the name of a larger synthesis. Significantly, his reflections upon the divine order he will reproduce in art lead to one of those transcendent ecstasies in which he is caught up into contemplation of pure Idea, of which Flaubert was so skeptical in the *Mémoires* and *Novembre*. The appearance of the dog, which literally haunts Jules, not only shatters that transcendent purity, but returns him to the particularity of a present reality.

L'Éducation sentimentale: Jules' Aesthetic Conversion

(whether real or hallucinated) and to a reflection upon his particular past. Unlike the smiling face of God behind the divine harmony he perceived in nature, the dog is an ambiguous creature, which sometimes resembles Faust's diabolical dog but which is also appealing and sympathetic. The relationship between Jules and the dog, a state of both fear and intimacy, Jules' acceptance that it belongs to some other domain than that of the tangibly real, is not necessarily proof of an external surreality in nature (another manifestation of the divine harmony). Rather, like the manifest content of a dream it refers to specific events in Jules' past which, because he can only intimate them through a masked symbolism, appear to remain a mystery, beyond deciphering.

It is not very difficult to find the event to which the episode of the dog refers. Jules himself tells us that the bridge to which the dog pulls him is the one where he was tempted to drown himself the day Lucinde left. Like a dream image, the dog has a multiple identity. Wolflike, abandoned, it represents the Jules who wandered like a mad wolf through the countryside. At the same time it is the little girl in rags (Jules prefers to call the dog "la bête" — which enables him to refer to it as "she") who begged for charity from him but whom he sent away because of his homicidal intentions. The body of Lucinde he sees in the river is the actualization of his desire to drown the little girl, which, of course, was an expression of his desire to drown Lucinde. Flaubert has embroidered what might have been a dream (and the archetype of the drowning figure is the drowning mother he describes in the dream in the *Mémoires*) with many artificial romantic devices. The dog itself is Mephistophelian, Ophelia mediates Lucinde, and the strange magnetic fluid that attaches him to the dog has Swedenborgian and Balzacian overtones. (One recalls that when Flaubert read Balzac's *Louis Lambert* he felt that Balzac was explaining his own experiences.) In spite of this phoniness, Jules' acknowledgment of the real connection between himself and the dog is not vitiated. It throws light on Flaubert's often expressed rapport between things, animals, and idiots, a rapport not due to magnetism but to a basic identification. As Sartre suggests, the appearance of the dog is a *totalization* of the past, but it is a totalization which, in spite of Jules' acceptance, remains unconscious.

L'Éducation sentimentale: Jules' Aesthetic Conversion

Without the episode of the dog Jules' new aesthetics would be based only on his desire that art should provide a magnificent synthesis between himself and the world. Flaubert rightly felt that such a radical change of direction needed some extraordinary validation, some convincing emotional base. But the episode of the dog is *after the fact*. Nor does it have anything to do with Jules' new aesthetics; it is a reaffirmation on a scarcely conscious level that his past lives and that, in spite of the opacity of the images in which it appears, he has a living connection with it. However, by turning it into a last manifestation of Jules' former romanticism, a visionary working-through of his false consciousness, Flaubert can validate Jules' conversion and validate his new aesthetics. Hence the absolute contradiction between Jules' emotional acceptance of the dog at the end of chapter 26 and his complete rejection of the experience at the beginning of the next chapter. There is no real logic between the acceptance of one's past and a pantheistic aesthetics, and the episode of the dog, with all its contradictions, points to the contrivance of the leap from the one to the other.

The point of departure of Jules' new aesthetics is the rejection of the romantic deformation of reality. On the simplest level, he asserts his new respect for the real by informing himself about facts. For instance, his romantic conception of America had led him to imagine that palm trees and lemon groves grew in New York; he corrects this misapprehension by a simple lesson in latitude and longitude. Similarly, he divests himself of the romantic cliché, the preference for the crooked over the straight, for purple cloaks and purple passages, for Venice, lagoons, lakes—with their eternal moonlight and "parties de barque." This mode of romanticism has become the property of the bourgeois, as Jules discovers when he hears a merchant falling into rapture over ruins for the memories they evoke and quoting the verse of Mme Desbordes-Valmore while he engraves his name on a stone, his heart "plein de poésie." He also rejects the fads of romantic literature, including the popular and folk revivals of savages, troubadours, and their contemporary, sentimental counterparts.

In order to train his taste away from these distortions, he begins the comparative study of various literary works, preferring

L'Éducation sentimentale: Jules' Aesthetic Conversion

those which clash with his "romantic" taste. And in order to make his own style more supple and muscular, he passes alternately from one school of style to another, hoping to effect a synthesis which would include the vitality of the Renaissance, the limpidity of the seventeenth century, the psychological and analytical insights of the eighteenth, and the poetry of the nineteenth, "qu'il sentait d'une autre manière et qu'il élargissait suivant ses besoins."

Beginning with the assumption of unity between man and nature, he no longer believes that language is inadequate to portray reality. Rather, form and matter are completely adequate to one another and develop in unison. However, he still conceives of language as a form (spirit) which absorbs and spiritualizes content (matter) in a "fusion divine où l'esprit s'assimilant la matière, la rend éternelle comme lui-même." Words are no longer, as they were for the narrator of the *Mémoires,* a fall from eternity, but they spiritualize matter into eternity. Although Jules completely reverses Flaubert's pessimistic conception of language, he maintains the same terms: eternity, spirit, matter.

Although all poetry creates its own rules, it emanates from an original source of light "dont le foyer est au sein de l'inconnu." Forms, therefore, are different modalities of a unique and absolute essence. The romanticism Flaubert demystified in the *Mémoires* and *Novembre* now reappears in another form—his love of the infinite has found an aesthetic validation. He no longer berates the artist for attempting to reproduce the inifinite but the critic for attempting to legislate works of art: "Et vous, vous voulez régler ce qui est la règle même, régir ce qui est la loi même, répartir au gré d'une symétrie extérieure toutes ces lueurs diverses, arrêter la création, la saisir par tous ses côtés, mesurer son avenir, compter tous les astres, peser l'infini" (p. 355).

The madman of the *Mémoires* attacked the bourgeois for believing that he could grasp the infinite by means of measurements and calculations. Jules, the artist, attacks the critics on the very same grounds. In both cases, the bourgeois and the critic are the reader, for whom the writer expresses a certain contempt. Jules' extravagant defense of the ineffability of the infinite, which was so prevalent in Flaubert's earlier works, should put us on guard

L'Éducation sentimentale: Jules' Aesthetic Conversion

against the so-called antiromanticism of his aesthetics.

Ceasing to believe in absolute aesthetic criteria, he sees theories and treatises on the Beautiful as reflective of specific historical situations and trends. He discovers that history is both more varied and more unified than he had thought and that the monstrous and the bizarre have their own laws just as do the graceful and pure. Again, he only repeats a romantic commonplace when he refuses to acknowledge that there is anything intrinsically ugly in nature. He recommends the impartiality of the scientist who studies with equal care the vertebrae of the boa and the larynx of the nightingale, and who transcends the notion of the ugly which exists only in the mind of man. All in nature is order and harmony, all forms emanate from the same womb and return to the same nothingness, rays of a single circle which converge towards the same center.

Since man is part of nature, he looks for a similar harmony in the moral sphere. And since the poet, above all, expresses not only himself but the whole of humanity, Jules examines works of art not only for their aesthetic and plastic qualities but for their general human significance. He simultaneously studies humanity in art and art in humanity—the harmony in the periodic repetition of the same crises and the same ideas, the coordination of cause and effect, the perfect functioning of what he calls a complete organism. This theory enables him to turn a scientific eye on history in which he only has to discern the underlying causes to understand its mechanism. Divesting himself of the current clichés affixed to various historical periods, he sees in it greater shading and variety. Obviously influenced by Montaigne, he finds inconsistencies in the most apparently consistent historical figures. For instance, he gives the case of Nero to show that this monster was nevertheless capable of weeping over the loss of an amulet given to him by his mother. Yet, unlike Montaigne, who quotes the example of Nero to highlight universal fluctuations of self and character, Jules concludes that such inconsistency proves man's basic mediocrity, in the most pejorative sense. In both good and evil, he is incapable of singlemindedness. Jules' apparent objectivity in his examination of history veils a bias to objectify and vilify man and offers a consolation for a great resentment: "Cette

L'Éducation sentimentale: Jules' Aesthetic Conversion

égalité continuelle de l'homme, quoi qu'il en ait et partout où il se trouve, lui semblait une justice qui rabaissait son orgueil, le consolait de ses humiliations intérieures, lui rendait enfin son vrai caractère d'homme et le replacait à sa place" (p. 356).

Jules' belief that nature contains all elements in a total unity permits him to find a place in his aesthetics for the fantastic. He cannot entirely explain the phenomenon, but as scientific observer he recognizes that its emergence in history occurs at the beginning and decline of cultures and civilizations. When he was a romantic, he confesses, he put too great an emphasis on the fantastic, but his lyrical effusions on the subject reveal that his passion for the fantastic has not waned. The fantastic, he suggests, acknowledges that ordinary language cannot express "les pensées qui ne se disent pas." Thus, he returns to the discrepancy between thought as a synonym for the infinite and words—to the fundamentally romantic assumption of the *Mémoires* and *Novembre*. Jules' romantic idealism masquerades as an objective rationality which accepts the romantic as a part of the infinite variety of nature: "On a besoin de tout ce qui n'est pas, tout ce qui est devient inutile. . . . Notre nature nous gêne, on y étouffe, on veut en sortir et notre âme qui l'a comblée, en fait craquer les parois comme une foule mal à l'aise dans une enceinte trop étroite." The fantastic is the expression not of the plenitude of all things but of the deficiency of nature, of man's negation of it in the name of nothingness. Attempting to explode natural boundaries, man puts on the mask of the monstrous and grotesque, goes mad, wallows in the ignoble in the hope of transcending matter, like the ascetic monk who whips himself until his increasing sensuality finally turns into a religious ecstasy. Flaubert has not given up his love of the infinite nor his basic dualism.

However, the distinction of great artists, according to Jules, is that they can reflect this infinite "comme se mire le ciel dans la mer." He conceives them as some extraordinary natural phenomenon, comparing their works to mountains which, as one tries to climb them, produce vertigo. They stand above all other men and even above their own suffering: "D'abord les hasards de la vie n'arrivaient pas jusqu'à eux." They can write equally well in jail or marching towards their death. Once again, this conception of

L'Éducation sentimentale: Jules' Aesthetic Conversion

the writer as being above all contingencies and separate from other men is romantic. He is genius, a god-created natural exception to the common run of men. Unsurprisingly, Jules designates Homer as the genius of the ancient world, Shakespeare of the modern. Both seem larger than life, both have eluded the definitions of the biographers. Like genius, inspiration is a divine gift which cannot be acquired by effort or will. And Jules/Flaubert disdainfully repeats what he wrote in the *Mémoires*: ". . . il se rappela le temps où il se battait les flancs pour se donner l'amour en vue de faire des sonnets" (p. 357). The function of the artist is to reveal the divine harmony in nature. And as Jules contemplates the works of the "immortals" he finds a total synthesis in which nothing is omitted and no detail is sacrificed to the whole: "Alors la suprême poésie, l'intelligence sans limites, la nature sur toutes ses faces, la passion dans tous ses cris, le coeur humain avec tous ses abîmes, s'allièrent en une synthèse immense dont il respectait chaque partie par amour de l'ensemble, sans vouloir ôter une seule larme des yeux humains ni une seule feuille aux forêts" (p. 358). He may have sacrificed the picturesque or petit-bourgeois romanticism, but he reaffirms the romantic pantheism which he had already questioned in the *Mémoires* and *Novembre*.

Obviously, the elaboration of Jules' new aesthetics radically interrupts the narrative flow of the *Éducation*. And when Flaubert has Jules go to Paris in order to study the human comedy, he does not advance the action of the novel. Rather, he is imitating a literary device in which Jules looks at the human comedy of Paris with the eyes of a foreigner, trying to understand the meaning of its absurdities. His insights into the contradictions and hypocrisies of the city recall Molière and Voltaire. One scene in particular imitates Candide's discovery of a Parisian salon where he meets an eloquent critic of the drama who turns out to be a playwright who has written one play that was hissed off the stage. Similarly, Jules finds himself in a salon where he is very impressed by the eloquence of a distinguished guest who turns out to be an unread novelist. This lack of originality should be sufficient to make the reader cautious about Jules' enthusiasm for his new aesthetics. Just as it resurrects Flaubert's old romanticism, it reaffirms on a particularly banal level the alienation between the artist and other

L'Éducation sentimentale: Jules' Aesthetic Conversion

men: if Jules prefers Burgundy, his host orders Bordeaux. His tastes in literature are not shared by others. His hatred of the cliché and bourgeois hypocrisy is only the other side, as was apparent in the *Mémoires* and *Novembre,* of a desire to transcend all language in a pantheistic unity. At the same time, the degrading irony Jules had specifically criticized at the time of his "conversion" reappears in his desire to destroy the memory of Lucinde. Thus, he meets Bernardi in Paris and takes particular pleasure in imagining her making love to him: ". . . quand il eut bien trainé dans la boue, retourné et rompu à toutes ses articulations le tendre et douloureux amour de sa jeunesse, et que la férocité de son esprit se fut repu de ce spectacle, il trouva moins de charme dans la société de Bernardi, et tout en continuant à le voir quelquefois, il lui paya moins souvent le café" (p. 362). This return to an irony which specifically aims at destroying the emotional reality of the past is a reminder that Jules' aesthetics does not so much arise from a personal insight as it denies that personal insight, just as he leaps from an acceptance of his experience with the dog to a complete rejection of it.

Flaubert reintroduces Henry in the last chapters of the *Éducation* almost as an afterthought. Jules and Henry meet in Paris, but they have completed their divergence from one another. Henry is the very opposite from Jules. He is an attractive chameleon who blends into the social background. When he describes Henry, Flaubert lapses into the clichés he so deplores in the mouths of the bourgeoisie. His language begins to break down, a process he awkwardly becomes aware of. Describing the grief of one of Henry's abandoned mistresses, he generalizes it and reduces it to a formula: ". . . leur chute en effet est multipliée par le carré de la vitesse." He justifies this facetiousness by explaining to the reader that he learned in his rhetoric class at school that one should embellish one's language with such flowers, so why should he not use a formula from physics, especially since it is the only one he knows, as a metaphor? The question itself is rhetorical but is a significant commentary on Jules' aesthetic ambitions. Having described art as the reproduction of infinity, he imitates Delille, who wrote verse about a coffeepot, and the poet who put the civil code into verse.

L'Éducation sentimentale: Jules' Aesthetic Conversion

The narrative voice begins to lapse into clichés and peremptory summaries as Flaubert hastens his novel to an end. Henry becomes nothing more than a caricature of the bourgeois. But while the characters become more and more drained of complexity and vitality, theories about the development of character still abound. Flaubert writes that Jules and Henry are the results of what they had been, since every day of their lives was a link in an indissoluble chain, and that it was Providence that determined the events that molded them. This determinism is another aspect of the pantheism in which every element in the ensemble has its predetermined place. Thus, it was the accident of Jules' unrequited love that determined his poetic consciousness, the accident of Henry's requited love that determined his integration into society.

Paradoxically, as the *Éducation* aesthetically collapses, Flaubert evokes Jules no longer as a struggling writer but as one of the "immortals" who has achieved his grandiose aesthetic vision. Jules, he tells us, has achieved the ultimate serenity of the great artist in the transcendence of his personal self. He has acquired the total pantheistic vision: "Il se pénètre de la couleur, s'assimile à la substance, corporifie l'esprit, spiritualise la matière; il perçoit ce qu'on ne sent pas, il éprouve ce qu'on ne peut point dire, il raconte ce qu'on n'exprime pas, il vous montre les idées qu'on ébauche et les éclairs qui surprennent; il va de l'oeuvre à l'inspiration qui l'a créée, et, rêvant à ces filiations diverses, comme un voile détaché qui court dans les cieux ou sur la surface bleue des mers, il flotte et remonte dans les espaces d'où elles sont parties, pour retrouver le sillon perdu de ces feux descendus sur la terre et la source cachée de ces effluves venus jusqu'à nous" (p. 370). But clearly, what Flaubert is describing has little to do with the act of writing. It is an invocation of the successful loss of will in a total identification with nature, an identification that he had sought in his earlier works but which had always yielded to a fall into the most opaque materiality. In this sense, Jules' vision is not a new discovery but a lapse into an old romantic indulgence. A successful Smahr, he claims to have found access to the mysteries of creation, to have discovered the original mold of all forms of life, the secret of their birth and decline, and their final purpose. Existence provides him with the accidental, he gives back

L'Éducation sentimentale: Jules' Aesthetic Conversion

the essential pattern. He receives the flux of the world and gives back the reflux of himself by means of art. And just as art offers no resistance to his identification with the cosmos, he finds no resistance between life and the idea, the clothing and the body. Conceiving of himself as a force of nature, he sees his genius as a mission and a fatality, and has joined the ranks of Homer and Shakespeare. However, he betrays the falseness of his claim to impartiality and indifference to audience in a metaphor in which he likens his state to that of a king on a throne receiving tributes and consoling himself for his solitude by the contemplation of the absurdities of the crowd beneath him. Jules has simply swept aside the tensions between language and the infinite, the problems of the creation of an original language, the inauthenticity of desires for power and revenge, of a hatred of men that masks itself as irony in the dream of losing himself in nature. There is no reality in his ideal vision, just as there is no reality in the imaginary characters. Jules imagines performing imaginary plays in an imaginary auditorium, and both afford him complete satisfaction.

While Jules celebrates his fulfillment as artist, Flaubert implicitly comments on its absurdity by letting his novel fall apart. *He* cannot transcend the cliché, *he* cannot pretend that his characters are anything more than puppets whose strings are pitifully evident, or that his novel is anything more than a lifeless mechanical contrivance. He asks his reader not to walk away from Jules and his enthusiastic raving until he has gathered his characters together on the stage for a final bow. The use of the metaphor of the theater in this context and the subsequent peremptory summing up of the destinies of the "actors" acknowledges the same failure as the inserted story in the *Mémoires.* The effort to create a narrative truth has lapsed into self-conscious manipulation. Place, action, and time have turned into empty reification.

It is strange that, given both the basis and consequence of Jules' aesthetics, it has so often been taken for Flaubert's first and last word about his aesthetic intentions. While it is undeniable that Flaubert's attack at Pont-l'Évêque radically changed the external conditions of his life and ultimately relieved him from pursuing a career in law—thereby giving him the chance of choosing art as a "necessity"—it does not then follow that Jules' aesthetics is any-

L'Éducation sentimentale: Jules' Aesthetic Conversion

thing more than a glorious wish for an art that would coincide with a total ecstatic passivity. Yet Jean Bruneau, for example, concludes that Jules' aesthetics shows that Flaubert has "definitively stepped outside of himself, he has become the perfect spectator, no longer being anything, he understands everything. His role is to explain to men the unity of the world into which he has had a grandiose intuition."[5] Similarly, Sartre interprets Jules' aesthetic leap as Flaubert's death to his childhood: "In '44 the child kills himself so that the old man can be born: ceasing to suffer, he changes his life into memory so as to make it into the reservoir for the imagination."[6] Obviously, Sartre's interpretation of this transformation has many pejorative overtones. Flaubert's aesthetics is equated with the denial of life and the refusal of self-definition.

In fact, Jules' aesthetics denies his original insight into the nature of reflection. By definition, it can never sum up, never have the last word. Jules' discovery of such reflection—properly speaking, *self*-reflection—occurs when he stops objectifying his experience by a mordant and reifying irony. He is not objective witness or passive medium of events, but he mediates the temporal process, creating a future through the reflective assimilation of the past. When he denies such self-reflection in the name of pantheism, he allows only for the temporality of a cause and effect existing in nature, in matter, even though it might be substantiated by some divine original cause.

Even critics like Georges Poulet and Jean-Pierre Richard, whose work has revolutionized criticism of Flaubert, have equated Jules with Flaubert. However, they are disturbed by the absence of a genuine subjectivity or temporality in Jules' aesthetics and make a heroic effort to reinterpret it from the perspective of Flaubert's total *prise de conscience*.

According to Poulet, the point of departure for Flaubert's aesthetic experience is the peculiar intensity which exists between the perceiving self and the object perceived, the origin of a "sentiment de l'existence."[7] Whereas the romantics meant by the expression "sentiment de l'existence" a feeling which transcended the perception of objects and gave rise to the emergence of an

L'Éducation sentimentale: Jules' Aesthetic Conversion

authentic self, Flaubert means by it the loss of the self in the objects of the external world: "All that remains is a unique being which can be indifferently called soul or nature."[8] By virtue of its intensity, this moment is brief, but Poulet identifies its duration with a Bergsonian becoming in which feeling, body, landscape, nature, life—all participate in the same temporal movement. With the lapse of this initial moment of sensation, Poulet continues, Flaubert has recourse to the memory of sensation in order to regain the initial intimacy. Thus, the interiorized sensation is the basis for a moment of total intimacy wholly in the present. However, whereas the sentiment of the external world is simple—the loss of consciousness in the pantheistic sense of the whole—the act of remembering is complex. One image rapidly stimulates another so that within the total intimacy there remains the awareness of the temporal distance between the different moments of the past that have been conjured up. Moreover, each image casts its reflection upon the image it in turn evokes and engenders an atmosphere peculiar to the act of remembering, the mood of the "real self." At the same time, the act of remembering creates a "depth in duration: The first memory is like the top of an incline; from there it is only possible to descend, to go down the slope, and to redescend this incline is to go through life again, to bring into consciousness the very thread of lived time. . . ."[9] As in the intense experience of sensation, the consciousness of the thread connecting past experiences reaches its limit in the revelation of temporal depth and extension. However, the inevitable moment of fall is more radical than that which follows an ecstasy based purely on sensation. It means the dissolution of the real self and the discovery of the past as a *néant*: thought "deprived of a future, devoured by the past, overwhelmed by the weight of the present," falls into the sluggish duration of meaningless repetition. No longer a rapid and meandering river, time becomes stagnant.

Thus Poulet sums up Flaubert's preliterary consciousness, the repetitive experience of an impasse which he would break through by means of literature. But on what is literature to be based? It is in the context of this question that Poulet interprets Jules' conversion.

L'Éducation sentimentale: Jules' Aesthetic Conversion

Poulet believes that the solution reached by Jules is the solution to Flaubert's torment at the temporal chaos of memory. Jules discovers that the ecstasy provoked by the revelation of the unity of past existence is the result of a deterministic order in the past, an inexorable consequence of cause and effect. This belief in causality provides the basis for a future act of writing in which the artist's function is to discover the laws of human behavior and the total design of nature.

Clearly, the structure of Flaubert's preliterary consciousness, as defined by Poulet, does not easily permit of a *logical* transition to Jules' belief in the objective truth and logical sequence of events. Indeed, from what we have already seen of the narrators of the *Mémoires* and *Novembre*, we know that Flaubert has already rejected the unity of the *sum* of experiences. Poulet rightly calls Jules' solution banal. But, in order not to convict Flaubert of a simplistic reliance on a transcendental order, Poulet interprets the system of cause and effect elaborated by Jules as an a posteriori construction, a movement away from sensation to cause and not from cause to sensation: "The first movement in Flaubert's reconstruction will be, therefore, an ascendant movement through which thought climbs, through a series of inferences, the ladder of causes, and thus moves away from the domain of sensation or actual images in order to pass into that of the order of things, into the domain of law."[10] And once patterns have been revealed, another moment of reconstruction follows, taking on the aspect of prospective representation, the making present of a vast effort of synthesis. According to Poulet, the Flaubertian periodic sentence embodies this double movement—from the present to the past, from the past to the present—in which "we find that from the protasis to the apodosis the different elements are composed in a rising and descending synthesis which, as it is completed, enables us to discover in the sentence an indissoluble unity in which everything becomes present. Henceforth the problem of time is only a problem of style."[11]

Poulet's complex reinterpretation of Jules' aesthetic theories avoids the error into which Bruneau and Sartre fall of suggesting that Flaubert's aesthetic attitude is that of objective spectator or passive medium of an external reality. He emphasizes the interi-

L'Éducation sentimentale: Jules' Aesthetic Conversion

ority of the aesthetic process and the essentially temporal nature of the act of writing which does not simply reflect a preexistent reality. However, while he may be correct in calling the individual Flaubertian sentence an indissoluble unity, a presentness made up of analysis and synthesis, he does not account for Flaubert's lifelong obsession with the problem of creating a unity between discrete sentences, a problem concerning narrative technique in its widest aspects. In fact, far from transforming the problem of time into a problem of technique, Flaubert's experiments with technique are major redefinitions of the temporality of the novel.

In his essay "La Création de la forme chez Flaubert,"[12] Jean-Pierre Richard takes the same point of departure as Poulet—the relationship between Flaubert and natural phenomena—but reaches a different conclusion. Whereas Poulet describes this relationship as one of brief but positive intimacy, Richard sees it as essentially negative. For him, Flaubert is ever on the verge of being swallowed up by objects, and his enormous appetite, both literal and figural, is the expression of his desire to negate these threatening objects by consuming them. In the world of reality, of course, such a project is inherently doomed to failure, for there is no possible resolution in the dialectic of appetite; the objective world can never be entirely assimilated. Fiction, however, according to Richard, permits Flaubert to distance himself from his negative relationship to the world of perception. It ceases to be his problem when it becomes that of his fictional characters. Every successful sentence and paragraph raises him a little from the "swamp" of the contingent self, creating a "solid" self only rarely glimpsed in his immediate experience of life. Moreover, his distance on his characters enables him to demystify all efforts to achieve transcendence outside of art. Thus, Madame Bovary represents the failure of achieving transcendence through sensation. Frédéric Moreau the failure of a platonic negation of sensation.

Richard equates Jules' disquiet at the fluctuations of his contingent self with Flaubert's disquiet at the fluid metamorphoses of self which provoked him to write his novels. But, like Poulet, he finds Jules' conventional determinism insufficient to explain the being of the aesthetic process. Writing is not Flaubert's way of losing his self but a way of revealing his inner self through a

L'Éducation sentimentale: Jules' Aesthetic Conversion

synthesis between *le mot juste* and the natural referent, between consciousness and experience. Words resume the past in a coherent present. Here Richard echoes Poulet's view that the perfect Flaubertian sentence is a plenitude, a total presence, the overcoming of division through a temporal synthesis.

However, whereas Poulet's definition of the Flaubertian sentence makes a fundamental distinction between natural and aesthetic processes, Richard's conception of *le mot juste* is not qualitatively but only quantitatively different from the anarchy of contingent reality. Typical metaphors he uses to describe the aesthetic transformation of experience are the hardening of the "mud of existence," or whipping cream into butter. He describes Flaubert's sense of solidarity with the past as that of "a rising thickness of existence which supports all the fluctuations of the present."[13] To "descend" into the past means, therefore, to plunge into an increasing impenetrability from which there is no issue. It is this very depth, according to Richard, which permits Flaubert to stay at the surface and recognize himself in the present. To write means to concentrate "on a single point and in a single moment all the solidity slowly accumulated and widely dispersed in the totality of space and time."[14] Writing recuperates all that which nature, instinct, and habit have accumulated in the depths of life. It is a recuperation of being. In the place of a preexistent determined order, it creates a design which hitherto did not exist. In spite of this correction to Jules' naive determinism, Richard's unfortunate use of metaphors for art as the hard crust of mud or as the butter arising from cream, suggest that the formless and the formal are part of the same unconscious organic unity. Jules' aesthetic theories thus represent a trap into which even the best critics of Flaubert have fallen.

Although Poulet and Richard are at first embarrassed by Jules' aesthetics, they not only incorporate it into Flaubert's aesthetics as a whole but give it a privileged place. Almost of necessity, therefore, they echo Jules' notion that art is the ultimate resolution of contingency and that "form" once and for all resolves the problem of time.

Jules' aesthetic conversion is indeed little more than an option for the same kind of pantheism about which Flaubert was so

L'Éducation sentimentale: Jules' Aesthetic Conversion

skeptical in the *Mémoires* and *Novembre*. The awkwardness and confusion surrounding this conversion cast their shadow on an aesthetics full of grandiose, wish-fulfilling delusions. The quite unreal transition whereby Flaubert moves from Jules' plans for a future work to the statement that the latter has in fact achieved the greatness of Homer and Shakespeare only highlights the evasive leap of Jules himself when, through the uneasy intermediary of the episode of the dog, he leaps from subjectivity to pantheism. What his aesthetics does reveal, however, is Flaubert's profound concern with the origin of and connection between forms—both in nature and art.

Jules' aesthetics is an attempt to make the laws of art subservient to the laws of nature, and he conceives the laws of nature as the laws of cause and effect. However, as we have seen in the letter to Louise Colet quoted in the introduction, Flaubert's criticism of the *Éducation* was based on the inadequacy of a simple structure of cause and effect: "The causes are shown, the effects too, but the linking between cause and effect is not. That is the vice of the book and its failure to live up to its title." Aesthetically, the book was full of gaps, several chapters should be revised or rewritten, and an entirely new chapter added. The new chapter, which would be the most difficult to write, would show how a trunk bifurcates, how one action rather than another brings about a change in character. Whereas, in the course of expounding Jules' aesthetics, he had said that a single cause—a successful or unrequited love, for example—produces a necessary effect—he is aware in his criticism of the novel that to give cause and effect is not enough, that what is important is the relation between cause and effect, the *linking* of the two. He thus repeats his criticism of the inserted story in the *Mémoires*: a description of external events fails to grasp existential development. In expressing the necessity of an added chapter in the *Éducation* which would bring about an appropriate linking between cause and effect, Flaubert might have had in mind the inadequately conceived leap of Jules' conversion, the most startling transition in the novel, which in fact prefaces the breakdown of the novel as novel. And in suggesting that the absence of linking between cause and effect belies the title of the novel, Flaubert reveals that what is lacking

L'Éducation sentimentale: Jules' Aesthetic Conversion

is the subjective experience, the *sentimental*—in its undistorted sense—mediation of events. Both Jules and Henry lack any authentic subjectivity and, since their voices are so commingled with the voice of the narrator, the novel itself inevitably lapses into empty poses, exemplified by Flaubert's acknowledgment that his characters—and ultimately himself—have become puppets on a stage.

As Flaubert indicates in his letter to Louise, the *Éducation* was an effort to reconcile his two distinct literary selves, the lyrical and the realistic. As he says, the effort failed, and it would have been easier to write two separate novels, the one entirely lyrical and the other entirely realistic. While Jules' aesthetics attempts to surmount duality by including every element of life within a natural unity, Jules excludes himself from the synthesis. He remains the dead observant eye of the totality—dead in that he no longer participates in any process of becoming. But such a deadness is not neutrality. Such a posture demands that the observed process be objectified—and consequently vilified. Jules' vilification of Lucinde is a coherent consequence of his aesthetics. Thus, while Flaubert considers the failure of the *Éducation* to be due to a dualism of plot and character, the realism of Henry versus the lyricism of Jules, in fact both heroes suffer from the same inaiblity to reconcile lyricism and realism. Henry moves from a lyrical romance with Mme Renaud to his cold-eyed arrivism and Jules moves from his passionate romanticism to a cold-eyed dissection of man. In acknowledging that the *Éducation* failed to accomplish a synthesis between realism and lyricism, Flaubert was only repeating what he had said in the *Mémoires* and *Novembre* about the difficulty of bringing together the voice of passionate enthusiasm and the voice of negative and destructive irony. But, as in the earlier works, the *Éducation* again points not to the duality between idealism and materialism but to their dialectical relationship. In spite of his suggesting that they should perhaps be treated in two separate works, Flaubert continually sketches out, while explicitly avoiding, a dialectical synthesis between the two. Thus, Flaubert denies the implied dialectical divergence in the characters of Jules and Henry when he dwells on Jules' aesthetics, which is based on a mechanistic structure of cause and effect analogous to that of natural phenomena. Implicit in such

L'Éducation sentimentale: Jules' Aesthetic Conversion

a dialectical movement is the moment of negativity which Flaubert awkwardly blurs in the *Mémoires, Novembre* and the *Éducation*. As is apparent in Jules' experience immediately preceding the episode of the dog, this moment of negativity corresponds to the discovery of the self as a being in time, the being which actively constitutes a future when it denies the reification of the past. Such a moment cannot be described as a plenitude, which Poulet and Richard would like to do, for it connotes a dizzying break with the world of contingency and a leap into an equally hazardous world of contingent forms. Flaubert's experiments with form in the *Tentation de saint Antoine, Madame Bovary, Salammbô,* the *Education sentimentale,* and *Bouvard and Pecuchet* clearly reveal that contingency is not solved by art, but that the limited forms of aesthetic expression only raise contingency to a higher level of problems.

If, as Flaubert said, a radical change took place in his life in 1844, the year of the crisis of Pont-l'Évêque, a change so radical and necessary that he called it mathematical, it was a change that meant his commitment to art. And Jules' particular aesthetic theories are important only in that they opt for art. Their content, however, is hardly the model for Flaubert's future aesthetics. In fact, it might be properly considered as a countermodel.

NOTES

1. See "The Significance of the Dog in Flaubert's *Éducation sentimentale*" by Marianne Bonwit, PMLA 42, no. 2 (June 1947): 517–24.
2. Bruneau, *Les Débuts.*
3. Ibid., p. 428.
4. *L'Idiot de la famille,* 2:1942.
5. *Lés Debuts,* p. 442.
6. *L'Idiot de la famille,* 2:1942.
7. Georges Poulet, *Études sur le temps humain* (Paris, 1950), pp. 308–26.
8. Ibid., p. 309.
9. Ibid., p. 313.
10. Ibid., p. 321.

11. Ibid., p. 324.
12. Jean-Pierre Richard, "La Création de la forme chez Flaubert," *Littérature et sensation* (Paris, 1964), pp. 196–243.
13. Ibid., p. 202.
14. Ibid., p. 239.

5

La Tentation de saint Antoine:
The Order of Fantasy

For all the justifications of realism in the aesthetics of the first *Éducation sentimentale,* Flaubert's next work of fiction, the *Tentation de saint Antoine* (1849), is his most fantastic.[1] It marks a return to the fantastic genre of his youthful short story "Un Voyage en enfer," and to the genre of the mystery play of *La Danse des morts* (1839) and *Smahr* (1838). The inspiration for these works is preeminently romantic—Goethe's *Faust,* Byron's *Cain,* and Quinet's *Ahasvérus*. It is not surprising, given this interest in the "ultimate mystery," that Flaubert, on a visit to Genoa in 1845, should have been particularly struck by his discovery of Breughel's painting of Saint Anthony. The painting not only recapitulated the themes of his own works but raised the problem of the meaning of fantasy, a problem that had become particularly acute since his experience of visual hallucinations at Pont-l'Évêque. Moreover, the painting recalled an intimate childhood memory: the performance of Saint Anthony and his temptations by the puppets of père Legrain at the annual fair of Saint-Romain in Rouen. The entire subject matter of the *Tentation* is Antoine's experience of fantasy. It therefore goes beyond the conventional form of the allegorical mystery play. It is a dream play, a play that in reality can never be performed.

In many ways the *Tentation* is Flaubert's most important work. It was, in fact, the first of his works he considered worthy of pub-

La Tentation de saint Antoine: The Order of Fantasy

lication. Unfortunately, its real celebrity does not reflect well on it. When he enthusiastically read the manuscript to his friends Louis Bouilhet and Maxime Du Camp, they unconditionally rejected it and advised him to treat a familiar, more everyday subject. Their advice led, of course, to *Madame Bovary*. However, Flaubert did not abandon his *Tentation*. He wrote a second version when he had finished *Madame Bovary* and another, the definitive version, after the *Éducation sentimentale*. This last version was published in 1874, when it provoked a very mixed critical response.

In spite of the three versions, the *Tentation* is really a single work. The last version overcomes the formal rigidity of the first two by intensifying the whirling and frenetic sequence of fantasies. It eradicates many of the abstractions and logical arguments of the earlier versions by replacing allegory with particularity and discussion with encounter. It also eradicates much of the facetiousness, typified by the mocking character of Antoine's pet pig, of the earlier versions. In other words, the last version is less profuse, less self-indulgent, and less mechanical.[2]

Much has been made of the comparison of Flaubert to a saint or hermit. It usually implies that he wished to withdraw from the world and, through the solitary and arduous discipline of art, attain to the absolute. Flaubert encourages this analogy by his own frequent comparisons of the artist to the saint. There are many such comparisons in Jules' aesthetics in the *Éducation sentimentale,* and they are reinforced by Flaubert's withdrawal from an "active" life after his nervous crisis. The label "the monk of Croisset" has become a cliché of literary history. However, it is a comparison that can be misleading. It suggests the successful accomplishment of the sacred enterprise of viewing the finite from the point of view of the infinite, the perspective assumed by Jules in the *Éducation sentimentale*. The relation between the finite and the infinite, the implicit theme of the *Mémoires, Novembre,* and the first *Éducation sentimentale,* takes on its most radical and explicit form in the *Tentation de saint Antoine.*

At the beginning of his dark night, Antoine longs to escape his ascetic discipline, the ritual of work and prayer, for the sensuous satisfactions of the world. But underlying this desire for pleasure

La Tentation de saint Antoine: The Order of Fantasy

is a much more serious temptation which emerges early in the drama. Thus, when the seductive queen of Sheba comes to tempt him, Antoine is able to resist her blandishments. He is much more fascinated by the magical arts of King Solomon and the idea that the world is an ensemble in which each part influences the whole, like the organs of the body. Solomon's purpose is to discover the principle that connects one part to the next, the principle of attraction and repulsion, so that he can modify the laws of nature to his own ends. This description of magic closely resembles Jules' theory of art in the *Éducation sentimentale,* which aims to understand the laws of nature in order to create a new synthesis. From the Christian point of view, Antoine's desire to uncover the secrets of matter represents a sinful curiosity and pride; from the aesthetic point of view, it remains to be seen how the *Tentation* modifies the aesthetics of Jules in the *Éducation sentimentale.*

The devil, masquerading as Hilarion, Antoine's former disciple, attempts to persuade the hermit to leave the desert and take up his place in the church establishment. Antoine replies that since man is spirit he should withdraw from all mortal preoccupations; all actions in the world are degrading. He himself resents being attached to the earth "even by the soles of his feet."

These two inclinations—to know the secrets of matter and to transcend matter—prefigure the pattern of Antoine's temptations. He veers between materialism and idealism in all their forms, looking for an absolute transcendence.

Hilarion skillfully parries Antoine's choice of solitude and withdrawal by pointing out that his so-called asceticism is only a refined self-indulgence. His solitary fantasies of love and power are not only more satisfying than reality but also the expression of contempt for and impotent hatred of the world. Through the mouth of Hilarion, playing analyst to Antoine, Flaubert demystifies his own predilection, evident in his youthful works, for the compensatory daydream. But Hilarion's purpose is to destroy Antoine's faith. He persuades him that what God most wants from man is the pursuit of truth and that, to this end, he should read everything written, not only the sacred texts, which are full of obscurities and contradictions. He promises to reveal to him the ultimate mysteries, the hierarchy of angels, the virtues and

La Tentation de saint Antoine: The Order of Fantasy

properties of numbers, the secrets of origin and metamorphosis. Antoine, who has already revealed his interest in magic, eagerly seizes upon the possibility of comprehending the absolute. He recalls that once he achieved through thought a moment of transcendence, but it was immediately followed by a fall. Now he avidly follows the path indicated by Hilarion: "Oui! Oui! ma pensée se débat pour sortir de sa prison. Il me semble qu'en ramenant mes forces j'y parviendrai. Quelquefois même, pendant la durée d'un éclair, je me trouve comme suspendu; puis je retombe." Slipping into a heretical dualism, he sees thought as a means to transcendence and matter as a restrictive prison.

According to Renan, many contemporary critics claimed that Flaubert had written, in the *Tentation,* a history of gnosticism and that a good précis would have sufficed. In fact, the inherent dualism of gnosticism reflects the central theme of the *Tentation;* its purpose is to transcend matter and reveal the divinity through intellectual knowledge. Matter is not the creation of God but of a demiurge and was therefore fallen from the beginning. Between God and creation is a series of intermediaries, divine beings arranged in pairs. An accident occurred in this celestial ladder which troubled the divine harmony and scattered divine sparks into the lower regions of creation. It is this divine spark which enables man to make the journey from sensation to pure spirit. The true Christ, in the gnostic system, is immaterial.

Besieged by crowds of gnostics with refined variations and versions of gnosis, Antoine is confused and overwhelmed. Each has something which interests him, but they contradict one another. According to Manes, the divine spark emerges more easily when stimulated by those material substances which most closely resemble the insubstantiality of thought: perfumes, spices, the bouquet of wines. Its emergence is hindered by all activity—even life-sustaining activity such as the killing of animals and the planting of crops. The implicit negation of life in the thought of Manes becomes explicit with Valentinus, who states that the most perfect of the eons is the Abyss which is paired with Thought. Intelligence and Truth, the Word and Life, Man and the Church, all finally derive from an original nothingness which is equated with thought. When the demiurge, who created matter, returns to the

La Tentation de saint Antoine: The Order of Fantasy

Plerôma, matter will devour itself in a final apocalypse and man will finally enter the Abyss of pure thought. Although Manes and Valentinus flee sensation, other gnostics maintain that the best way to transcend matter is by extreme indulgence in it. The disciples of Carpocrates, Nicholas, Marcos, and Helvidius, therefore advocate every kind of sensual indulgence. Thus, as we saw in the apparent polarity between the narrator of *Novembre* and the prostitute (the chastity of the one contrasted with the sensuality of the other), the spiritualism and materialism of gnosticism both aim, through divergent paths, for a transcendent unity.

Although Antoine is confused by the strange practices of the gnostics, he is forced to recognize that their moral strength equals, and even surpasses, that of Christians. In the cells of the Roman martyrs, one man alone, a disciple of the gnostic Montanus, advances passively, but with equanimity, to his death. The Christians quake with fear. In an adjacent scene, Antoine watches the relatives and lovers of the Christian martyrs lamenting over the tombs of their dead, but their lamentations turn into cries of pleasure as they flee the consciousness of death in an orgy of the flesh.

The gnostic quest for transcendence and its implicit negation of reality reaches a climax in the gymnosophist whom Antoine discovers on a funeral pyre, preparing to immolate himself. After a long period of reflective immobility, the gymnosophist has succeeded in negating all forms and even thought itself. Having reached a state of nothingness, he is about to enter the universal soul, the state of absolute nothingness. He knows neither hope nor anguish, happiness nor despair, day nor night. He has shed sensation, perception, knowledge in an ultimate weariness of the various bodily forms he has assumed in his journey towards spiritual perfection. The body was the prison of the spirit, and once the body disappears, the spirit immediately negates itself.

The gymnosophist represents the possibility of transcendence through the negation of all forms, but Antoine returns to the possibility, implicit in his reflections upon Solomon, of the control of forms through the knowledge of the secrets of nature. He encounters Simon the magician accompanied by Ennoia (an erstwhile eon in the hierarchical system of Valentinus), who tempts

La Tentation de saint Antoine: The Order of Fantasy

him with the secrets of natural metamorphoses. Because of the jealousy of the divine powers, Ennoia was cast from the celestial order into matter, where she took the form of Helen of Troy, Lucretia, Delilah, the daughter of Israel, and, finally, the eternal prostitute. Simon claims that his power has restored Ennoia to her original spiritual perfection. She is Minerva to his synthesis of Jupiter, Apollo, Christ, the Paraclete. He is capable of effecting any transformation of form, of animating bronze serpents, making marble statues laugh, dogs talk; he can walk on clouds and sea, pass through mountains, change his age, take on animal form, control the elements. Recalling that Simon was unmasked by the apostles of Christ, Antoine dispels him only to be confronted by a much more formidable sage and magician, the Greek Apollonius of Tyana.

Apollonius has a total knowledge of all the gods, all rites, all prayers, and all oracles. Like Christ, he can perform miracles and has achieved the highest expression of moral perfection. He offers to reveal to Antoine the ultimate mysteries, the reason for the various forms of the gods, and the world of Ideas behind forms: the Word, the Eternal, Absolute Being. But Antoine clings to the earth and to the truth of his own God as Apollonius, inviting him to accompany him in the final flight, steps over the edge of the precipice and rises into the air.

However, Apollonius has inflamed Antoine's curiosity about the various and multiple forms the gods assume. Antoine recalls that when he lived in the temple of Heliopolis he was fascinated by the supernatural figures painted on the walls: vultures carrying scepters, crocodiles plucking lyres, serpents with the faces of men, women with the heads of cows, bowing before ithyphallic gods. They awoke in him reveries on other worlds. He concludes that these strange forms must contain a spirit in them, that, in some strange way, the soul of the gods is inseparable from their images. However, when the most primitive forms of gods pass before him—shells, stones, branches of trees, vague representations of animals, hydropic dwarfs—he bursts out laughing at the idea that such forms could contain anything divine. But as the gods take on more recognizably human form, he becomes enraged. Under the insinuations of Hilarion, he is forced to doubt

La Tentation de saint Antoine: The Order of Fantasy

the exclusive truth of his own God, manifest in the figure of Christ. Like the other gods, his own demands sacrifices and the performance of exorcism and has no monopoly, as Antoine has seen with the gnostics, on morality or virtue.

Antoine is completely dazzled by the continual metamorphoses of the gods, which reach a climax in the transformations of the Indian gods which, as Hilarion explains, paradoxically express the Brahmins' belief that a primordial duality will ultimately be resolved in the absence of form, the Absolute. From the navel of a young god, cradled in a boat of serpents on an endless lake of milk, springs a lotus in which there are three other gods, and then three others and so on, endlessly. The gods couple and multiply; fountains spring from their heads, grass grows from their nostrils; all forms merge in a chaos of dancing, pursuit, meditation, exotic animals, streamers, tents. The connection between these forms and what they spiritually represent remains absurd. For instance, a god with an elephant's trunk, scratching his abdomen, is the solar god and inspirer of divine wisdom. However, every natural phenomenon—the winds, the planets, the months, the days—has its own god which undergoes incessant metamorphosis for the purpose, Hilarion explains, of maintaining equilibrium and combating evil. Like natural forms, the forms of the gods wear out; hence the necessity for continual renewal.

This continual metamorphosis is not purposeless, however. Buddha comes to announce that he has achieved the ultimate manifestation, the final period has been fulfilled. He recounts his Christlike life, his temptations in the wilderness, his various forms—all leading to the last existence in which nothing remains to be accomplished and form can return to nothingness. With this announcement, the gods fade and fall into the abyss.

As in gnosticism, the fantastic forms of the gods are only stages on the journey from matter to pure spirit, nothingness. And, as also in gnosticism, when the spiritual journey has been completed, there is a final apocalypse of matter. Antoine witnesses the passing of the gods, Oannes—the consciousness of Chaos who gave coherent shape to the formless, to scattered fingers, fins, and wings, eyes without heads—the goddesses of nature and fertility, the ancient gods of Egypt, the entire Greek pantheon. Apollo makes a

La Tentation de saint Antoine: The Order of Fantasy

last effort to find inspiration and create sublime poems in which all matter will be penetrated by the vibrations of his cither. But the strings break, and he throws his instrument away in the name of pure idea: "Non! assez des formes! Plus loin encore! Tout au sommet! Dans l'idée pure" (p. 561). But he becomes tangled in his broken chariot and falls headlong into the abyss. Apollo's desire to transform matter through poetry runs counter to the rampant dualism between matter and spirit of the gnostics and Buddha, but he too succumbs to the desire to transcend all form in pure idea which, inevitably, turns out to be pure nothingness. With the death of the gods, including the god of the Old Testament, there remains only Hilarion, the incarnation of the devil. The death of the gods, a common theme of romantic and symbolist literature, leaves a void between Matter and Idea. There are no longer any mediating forms.

The devil's kingdom is that of intellect. He enlarges the mind and weighs worlds without fear, pity, or love. As he says, and Flaubert has in mind the particular modern application of the word, he is Science. Assuming the vantage point so common in Flaubert's early writing, the devil takes Antoine high up into the atmosphere from where he has a total view of the world. He shows him that the heavens are empty of the divine. Antoine becomes excited by the principles and laws that govern the universe, the attractions and repulsions of the stars, and wishes to understand the nature of infinity. But after the initial excitement of perceiving constellations never before seen and discovering complex calculations, he fails to see the purpose of it all. Whereupon the devil informs him that it has no purpose. What appeared to be a void is nothing but interminable matter, a conception which fills Antoine with a greater vertigo than the conception of the abyss. Moreover, since Antoine's perception of the world is structured by his finite mind, he must admit that his perspective is limited and deformed. Thus, the devil leads him to wonder whether form is not merely an error of his perception, substance a fantasy, and reality a complete illusion. Once again trapped by the vicious circle of pure materiality versus pure insubstantiality, Antoine falls into complete despair where he has to choose between the ultimate pair of dualities, life and death, Eros and Thanatos.

La Tentation de saint Antoine: The Order of Fantasy

They engage in a battle for his soul, death urging him to suicide, lust to the pleasures of the flesh. However, what they promise him is the same annihilation. And, far from being in opposition, Antoine concludes, they are inseparable. Death is necessary for the continuation of life; therefore it does not really denote a void but a stage in a material process. But if substance is unique, he wonders, why is there such diversity of form? He muses that somewhere there must exist a primordial form which is body and image at the same time. If he could *see* such a form, he would know the link between matter and thought, the nature of Being. He recalls such primordial figures painted on the walls of the temple of Baal; he believes he has even glimpsed them flying over the desert which is familiar with animal forms that defy the imagination. And then he witnesses the struggle between the sphinx and the chimera to join together. Each wants to possess the other, but the enigma of the sphinx cannot be reconciled with chimerical flights of fancy. These figures do not effect the synthesis Antoine is looking for. Finally, however, he witnesses the amazing procession of primeval forms that lead him to the original form. As the first group explains, they are a little more than dreams but not quite beings. The second group have only half a body and live in half a house with their half children; the third have no head; the fourth are pygmies; the fifth are held to the ground by their hair, which has taken root. After these fantastic peoples Antoine witnesses a procession of fantastic animals —the griffin, the unicorn, and birds who live on air. As the animals become more primitive, the scene changes to the ocean and to the forms of shellfish, jellyfish which are hardly distinguishable from sponges, sea anemones, and polyps, plants which resemble insects, and insects which resemble flowers. Finally, in fragments of ice, he discovers the fossils of bushes and shells but cannot tell whether they are the imprint of those things or the things themselves. Diamonds shine like eyes; minerals palpitate. And he loses all his fear as he discovers the point at which all forms fuse and originate: little globular masses as small as the head of a pin and encircled by ciliae. In delirium he rejoices at seeing the origin of all life. He wishes to be part of the palpitating mass. He wants to fly, swim, bellow, howl, to have wings, a shell,

La Tentation de saint Antoine: The Order of Fantasy

a bark—to divide himself into everything, to grow like plants, flow like water, penetrate every atom, and to descend to the center of matter to *be* matter.

After this extraordinary experience the day dawns, and in the disk of the sun is the face of Christ. Antoine makes the sign of the cross and begins to pray.

Antoine's desire to discover a primordial form in which he would discover the link between matter and thought is satisfied by the realization that apparently insubstantial, dreamlike forms have a purely material origin. As in Jules' aesthetics in the *Éducation sentimentale,* Antoine overcomes the dualism between spirit and matter, the void and substance, in the unity of a great chain of being in which all forms have a material rationale. Whereas Jules can only say that all forms radiate from a single center, without naming the center, Antoine describes it as the living cell. In fact, it is not hard to find the nineteenth-century equivalent of the living cell. In 1860 Flaubert became familiar with that Darwinian principle of life and growth when he read Pouchet's *Hétérogène, où de la génération spontanée.* And just as Jules wishes to lose himself in his creation, the reflection of the larger unity, Antoine wishes to lose himself in material creation. Having found how forms are linked one to another, they wish, like the magicians Solomon and Simon, like Apollonius and Buddha, to get into the skin of different forms of being. Thus, the self is negated and eternity guaranteed.

The *Tentation* appears not only to resolve the conflict between idealism and materialism but also to explain the nature of the fantastic. In the *Éducation* Jules cannot completely account for the fantastic but acknowledges that it has a part in the grand design of nature and history. However, he states that nothing beautiful can come from the gratuitous invention of animals or plants which do not exist—by giving a horse wings and a woman the tail of a fish. These impossible existences, revelations of an ungraspable type, dreams without bodies, offering only the aspect of the vague desire which created them, remain isolated from one another in immobility and impotence. Although he cannot explain the many manifestations of the fantastic, he concludes that it expresses man's unquenchable appetite for more life and for the in-

La Tentation de saint Antoine: The Order of Fantasy

finite. Moreover, the supernatural can be historically situated at the beginning and decadence of civilizations. From the point of view of Jules' psychological and historical interpretation of the fantastic, the *Tentation* describes the personal pathology of Antoine against the background of the social pathology of fourth-century Alexandria with its corruption and religious and philosophical eclecticism—a period Flaubert liked to compare to his own century.

Flaubert appears to anticipate Antoine's materialist explanation for fantasy in *Par les Champs et par les grèves*. On a visit to a museum of natural history, the sight of monstrous Siamese-twin pigs, and of an equally monstrous human foetus, leads him to reflect on fantastic forms. Although they might represent a special form of aesthetic harmony, they are part of a gradated order of beings that originates in the unknown. He makes no radical distinction between physical and imagined monsters, since both are "rêves de la nature." Like metals, rocks, and rivers, the universe of fantasy—he gives the monsters of Greek mythology as an example—developed slowly, drawing itself from the *néant* by its internal force. With anxious amazement, he wonders whether his own thoughts cohabited in a common country with "those thoughts that have become forms," whether the principle of his own form originated in the universal chrysalis, "la chrysalide universelle," with the seed of the oak and the stream that fed the sea. Although Flaubert here integrates fantasy into the material order, the status of that material order remains ambiguous. It alternately originates in the unknown and in nothingness (which Flaubert identifies with the "thought" that precedes form) or in a material cell, the universal chrysalis which obviously anticipates Antoine's "cellule scientifique." It raises the question, which is prior, the Idea or the form? If the Idea is prior, then the forms, both physical and fantastic, are only appearances; if matter is prior, then thought and fantasy must have their source, the same source, in matter.

Antoine faces this same question at the end of the *Tentation* with the alternate temptations of absolute nothingness, the domain of pure reflection, and absolute materiality. He succumbs to the temptation of materiality. There is no nothingness, only

La Tentation de saint Antoine: The Order of Fantasy

the infinite extension of matter in which thought also has its source. He therefore overcomes the apparent dualism between idealism and materialism by opting for materialism. The Idea has its origin in matter.

Flaubert makes it clear in his unpublished notes to the *Tentation* that the material cell is the ultimate revelation. It is both Matter and Being, the origin of all forms, and the eternal: "... après le sphinx et la chimère les animaux antédiluviens, informes et peu à peu arriver par une série de monstrosités (symbolique) à la cellule vivante, à l'Être, à la matière. Ainsi St. Antoine a remonté l'échelle,—et il atteint ce qui est primitivement, éternellement."[3] Even here, where Flaubert plainly states that Antoine witnesses the devolution of forms to their common material origin, he parenthetically introduces the disturbing word "symbolic." Superficially, he means that he is representing more and more primitive forms of life by these monstrous forms, but he raises the question whether symbolic form can really be assimilated to material form. If the products of the mind and matter have the same origin, why bother to distinguish a literal from a symbolic progression? As in *Par les Champs et par les grèves,* Antoine's resolution of mind and matter appears rather quixotic.

Nevertheless, given the approximations to Antoine's material vision in Flaubert's other works, it is tempting to interpret it as Flaubert's own. Thus, in his essay "Saint Antoine et les monstres" Jean Seznec writes: "Thus, what the monsters reveal to Flaubert is what Saint Antoine anxiously seeks for: the principle behind the continuity of creation. Not only do they open up the mysterious dispensary in which the infinite diversity of forms is elaborated; but they also make it possible to understand how these forms are related to one another."[4] Thought and matter, flights of fancy, and material facts belong to the same evolving chain of being. Seznec does not indicate how this discovery might apply to the interpretation of the *aesthetic* structure of the *Tentation,* but Alfred Lombard, who starts from the same premise as Seznec, reaches the obvious aesthetic conclusion. The identity between matter and form as perceived by Antoine, he writes in his *Flaubert et saint Antoine,* can be taken as the basis of Flaubert's aesthetics, the purpose of which is to discover by a close examination

La Tentation de saint Antoine: The Order of Fantasy

of causes the necessary connections between phenomena. Aesthetic order thus naturally imitates the inherent harmony and coherence of an original psychological and historical matter. From this perspective, the fantastic demonism and the extraordinary lyricism of the *Tentation,* which Lombard himself calls a poetic reverie, can be reduced, as any other psychic phenomenon, to scientific explanation: "The extraordinary fact of demonic temptation has left poetic reverie and sacred legend and entered scientific truth; it is amenable to literary realism just like any other psychological experience furnished by history or the observation of manners. A scientific poem of the Christian supernatural, the *Tentation* was also, became, particularly with the development of Flaubert's genius, the historical poem of the decline of ancient thinking."[5]

However, finding Antoine/Flaubert's discovery of the scientific cell congenial to the premises of literary positivism, Seznec and Lombard fail to take into serious account that Flaubert considers Antoine's capitulation to the primacy of matter to be his ultimate temptation and his greatest error. Flaubert makes this very clear in his notes to the *Tentation* in which he associates Antoine's desire to be matter with the victory of the devil: "1. défilade / 2. tourbillon d'action / Antoine / tentation—veut être matière le diable / (l'emporte)"[6] In fact, the devil's laughter closes the first two versions of the *Tentation,* and the Christian apotheosis which culminates the third is not a benediction on Antoine's desire to be matter but the gift of grace bestowed on Antoine when he has plumbed the depths of his weakness. As de Goncourt records in his *Journal* (18 October 1872), Flaubert told him that he meant Antoine's fascination with the living cell, the "cellule scientifique," to be the sign of his greatest defeat: "Flaubert confides to me that the saint's defeat is due to the cell, the scientific cell." Goncourt was astonished by this confidence, but Flaubert was equally astonished by his friend's astonishment.

Antoine's desire to be matter is the culmination of a developing loss of will and ego. In the course of his temptations he becomes increasingly passive, one might almost say imbecilic. But, from the point of view of Christian orthodoxy concerning saintliness, this is how Flaubert wished him to be. He writes in his

La Tentation de saint Antoine: The Order of Fantasy

notes that he aims to create a general tone of idiocy and fatigue on the part of the saint, and quotes a page from George Sand's novel *Mademoiselle de la Quintinie* in which Father Onorion describes the first stage of saintliness for the ascetic as that of becoming a thing, "the thing of God," no longer capable of either sin or merit. Temptation demands a kind of resignation, a stupidity which is at the same time a hard resistance against sin and the devil. The final stage in the journey towards saintliness is reached only by virtue of divine grace. Antoine's basic reaction to temptation is passive, and, until his desire to be matter, his resistance against the devil is successful. But when he finally wishes to become a thing, to enter a scientifically conceived order of nature, he momentarily forgets God. But, paradoxically, as he is furthest away from God, so is he closest to salvation. The length and depth of his ordeal and his loss of a personally differentiated self make it possible for the gift of grace to occur. The ending of the *Tentation* is therefore necessarily gratuitous.

However, in spite of Seznec's and Lombard's failure to take into account Flaubert's implicit and explicit critique of materialism in the content of the *Tentation,* still, his rigorous historical and psychological research into the background of fourth-century Alexandria and its philosophical extravagances would tend to support their view that the aesthetic rationale of the *Tentation* can be found in psychological and historical realism. Still, the form of the *Tentation* raises a number of problems.

The few critics who have commented on the aesthetic structure of the *Tentation* have above all noted the significant lack of unity and continuity of the work. In fact, in his witty essay "La Tentation de (saint) Flaubert," Paul Valéry attributes this lack of unity precisely to Flaubert's persistent use of psychological and historical data.[7] In his view, the mass of data which freights each episode of the *Tentation* destroys the existential truth of Antoine's experience. It thereby causes the work to limp along and inhibits its creative possibilities: "Flaubert seems only to have glimpsed what the subject matter of the *Tentation* offered in terms of incentives, pretexts and opportunities for a truly superior work. His scruples about exactitude and references only showed up what he lacked in decision and purpose of composition in the

La Tentation de saint Antoine: The Order of Fantasy

command over the fabrication of a high-powered literary machine."[8] The *Tentation* fails, therefore, for the lack of a unifying purpose or perspective. The correct perspective, according to Valéry, should have been that of the saint, but the perspective of the scholar Flaubert persistently intrudes and turns the work into "a diversity of moments and pieces." Thus, Antoine, like the animated figures of père Legrain, remains a mere puppet, and we can see Flaubert manipulating the strings.

Valéry's remarks on the aesthetic disproportion of the work are very astute, but it is difficult to see how Antoine, who by definition is a passive thing in a demonic and divine plot, could have constituted an active existential focus. He is not, after all, a Monsieur Teste, for whom the drama of consciousness constitutes its own vital unity and purpose. Antoine's fantasies may originate in his own mind, but they become radically separate from him; he is manipulated by them. Thus, Valéry forces us to ask whether it is Flaubert's scholarship which overburdens Antoine or whether it is the latter's alienated imagination.

Victor Brombert also remarks on the lack of unity in the *Tentation*. However, he suggests that the diversity of moments and pieces is a deliberate "tool of disjunction" which Flaubert uses to express his main theme, "the horror of unending discontinuity." In his view, the dizzying, shifting tableaux express the impossibility of reconciling desire and the satisfaction of desire, the metaphysical counterpart of the failure of Emma Bovary's romanticism and Bouvard and Pécuchet's scientific empiricism. At the same time, however, he interprets the excesses of the *Tentation* as a reflection of Flaubert's psychological and cultural distortions: "In part [Flaubert's] concern with excess and massive accumulation of phenomena must be related to a social and cultural diagnosis, to a denunciation of the sanguine arrogance of bourgeois society of which Flaubert felt himself simultaneously the critic and the accomplice. But to an even greater degree, it does point to a form of self-denunciation, to the mythopoeic diagnosis of a private disease, the tragic combination of gigantic yearnings and fundamental debility."[9]

However, fragmentation was not, as Brombert suggests, Flaubert's aesthetic intention. Like Antoine, Flaubert was obsessed

119

La Tentation de saint Antoine: The Order of Fantasy

by the desire to discover how forms are related to one another. But, on the aesthetic level, it was up to him to find the unifying principle. As soon as he began the *Tentation*, he was tormented with the problem of ordering and connecting Antoine's fantasies. However reluctantly, he agreed with Du Camp's verdict that the first version, at least, was a failure: "De ce que j'avais beaucoup travaillé les éléments matériels du livre, la partie historique je veux dire, je me suis imaginé que le scénario était fait et je m'y suis mis. Tout dépend du plan. *Saint Antoine* en manque. La déduction des idées sévèrement suivie n'a pas son parallélisme dans l'enchaînement des faits. Avec beaucoup d'échafaudages romantiques, le dramatique manque."[10] He admits that he originally believed that the elaboration of the historical material and the philosophical content of Angoine's fantasies would be sufficient to guarantee the unity of the work. But he found that the material elements of the work provided so much scaffolding but no dramatic continuity. The result was a disproportion between ideas and drama. What was lacking was a scenario. He was not satisfied with the second version and he was still grappling with the plan when he came to the third: ". . . je refais un nouveau plan . . . j'espère parvenir à trouver un lien logique (et partant un intérêt dramatique) entre les différentes hallucinations du saint."[11] He found that no matter how he might connect the historical ideas of the *Tentation*, it was still difficult to connect Antoine's hallucinations in a dramatic way. He was facing the aesthetic problem Jules raises in the *Éducation sentimentale* with respect to the creations of fantasy, namely, "these bodiless dreams" remain isolated from one another in impotent immobility. No matter how Antoine attaches fantasy to the unified continuity of matter, the problem of creating an aesthetic "enchaînement" between fantasies persistently remained.

The theater was Flaubert's first and greatest passion. As a child of ten he composed and acted in his own (heavily plagiarized) plays and commandeered his friend Alfred Le Poittevin and his sister Caroline as supporting cast. He continued to write scenarios all his life, but the plays that he completed are stiff and lifeless. Only one, *Le Candidat,* was ever performed (in 1874, the same year as the publication of the *Tentation*). In the face of a unani-

La Tentation de saint Antoine: The Order of Fantasy

mously negative response, Flaubert withdrew it from the stage after only four performances. However, although the *Tentation* is a drama, and Flaubert speaks of the necessity of creating a coherent scenario and dramatic continuity between scenes, it defies representation on a physical stage. In fact, he specifically writes in his notes: ". . . enlever tout ce qui peut rappeler un théâtre, une scene, une rampe."[12]

It is ironic, given this desire to break down the boundaries of an artificial stage, that Flaubert apparently describes the initial setting of his drama with a conventional, physical stage in mind. The scene is the top of a mountain in the Thebaid, which Flaubert calls a "platform" and which is closed to the "left" and "right" by large stones. Like a backdrop, the sand of the desert rolls into the distance, and at the front of the stage a palm tree hangs over the abyss of the steep mountain at the foot of which runs the Nile. He describes in detail the physical properties of the hermit's cabin and the objects belonging to Antoine. And he also seems to have a director in mind when he indicates that there is a cross "ten paces" from the cabin. This description is written from an imaginary third-person point of view and places the reader in the position of watching the saint's drama from a distance. However, the effects of the fading light transform this artificial reality into a mirage, the image of Antoine's consciousness. The sun's rays darken, the blue of the sky takes on the color of mother-of-pearl, the bushes, stones, and earth appear to be as hard as bronze; and in the air floats a golden dust so fine that it merges into the vibrations of the light. This strange light produces an "aura" which announces the insubstantial reality of Antoine's hallucinations.

Since hallucinations are subjective impressions, Flaubert thought he could unify them by grounding them in Antoine's biography, that is, by giving their psychological source. When he wrote in his notes that "tout doit être réaliste," he meant that he must give Antoine's fantasies psychological versimilitude. Moreover, since these hallucinations are also expressions of Antoine's desires, they reveal what he already anticipates: ". . . faire que St Antoine pense les péchés plutôt qu'il ne les voit—ou mieux avant de les voir."[13] Thus, Flaubert establishes a possible princi-

La Tentation de saint Antoine: The Order of Fantasy

ple of continuity between them by relating Antoine's hallucination to his memories and desires.

In his opening soliloquy, from the perspective of boredom with his daily routine of work and lack of inspiration for prayer, Antoine recalls the past. Each detail of this past prefigures the content of his hallucinations. His mother and Ammonaria are the prototypes for the women of the *Tentation* and most explicitly of death and lust; his wandering in the desert, where he sought shelter in caves and tombs and was prey to natural threats and imaginary fears, prefigures the fantastic shapes which come to torment him. His studies in Alexandria form the basis for his intellectual and heretical temptations. His authority over other anchorites prefigures his ambitious and worldly desires. Antoine will refer to such biographical details at various points during the course of his hallucinations. Thus, before the procession of the gods he recalls the paintings of gods on the wall of the temple of Heliopolis, and before the procession of the monsters, the strange shapes painted on the walls of the temple of Baal. His reflections on his mother and the sensual Ammonaria immediately precede the appearance of the old and young woman who embody death and lust. Also, his intellectual and philosophical temptations are preceded by an expressed curiosity. And the devil himself takes on the form of an old disciple, Hilarion.

For the same purpose of psychological verisimilitude, Flaubert builds up Antoine's fantasies in a gradual way: *"Observer partout une gradation psychologique"* (Flaubert's italics).[14] Antoine's own consciousness must transform reality, and so gradually that he will be unaware of the transformation: "Tant les visions ont eu des gradations de netteté."[15] The first image which reflects Antoine's change of consciousness is the hallucinatory aura which opens the drama. As he reflects on his past, he gradually begins to forget where he is, and the natural scenery around him undergoes a gradual metamorphosis. Birds flying by seem to form a triangular battalion, like a piece of metal shimmering at the edges. The birds' wings remind him of the sails of the long boats and then of the visitors who would return home on the boats of the Nile. This image leads him to dream of far-off places and to long for the company of his visitors and the little gifts which would

La Tentation de saint Antoine: The Order of Fantasy

palliate his solitude. This movement into fantasy originates in an original metaphor, that of birds' wings resembling sails, and proceeds by a series of associations. Hoping to distract himself from his dreams by opening the Bible, Antoine finds only a further source of temptation. For instance, reading about Solomon, he muses on the wonders of the science of magic and finds that the shadows of the cross seem to be projecting two large horns. Once again he returns to a soliloquy in which he laments his loneliness and poverty, aware, however, that his faint-heartedness might be due to the literal faintness brought on by hunger. It is in this state of physical and mental exhaustion that Antoine begins to confuse reality and the imagination. Dreaming of the penitent women who used to visit him, he calls out to them and confuses the echo of his own voice with their response, a voice tempting him with women, money, and power. At this point the old palm tree turns into the torso of a woman, her long hair swaying over the abyss. Antoine's fantasies still have an imitative relation to the natural object. The devil's horns literally resemble the shadows cast by the cross, the torso of the woman resembles the shape of the palm tree; but in a climactic moment they suddenly take on an autonomous reality and intrude incoherently upon the scene.

Flaubert calls upon his intimate knowledge of hallucination in describing Antoine's complete loss of consciousness and the explosion of fantasy. Simple metaphorical associations between fantasy and reality break down, images proliferate chaotically, severing all connection with Antoine's surroundings and finally with Antoine himself: "Et, tout à coup, passent au milieu de l'air, d'abord une flaque d'eau, ensuite une prostituée, le coin d'un temple, une figure de soldat, un char avec deux chevaux blancs qui se cabrent. Ces images arrivent brusquement, par secousses, se détachant sur la nuit comme des peintures d'écarlate sur de l'ébène. Leur mouvement s'accélère. Elles défilent d'une façon vertigineuse. D'autres fois elles s'arrêtent et pâlissent par degrés, se fondent; ou bien elles s'envolent, et immédiatement d'autres arrivent. Antoine ferme ses paupières. Elles se multiplient, l'entourent, l'assiègent. Une épouvante indicible l'envahit; et il ne se sent plus rien qu'une contraction brûlante à l'épigastre. Malgré le vacarme de sa tête, il perçoit un silence énorme qui le

La Tentation de saint Antoine: The Order of Fantasy

sépare du monde. Il tâche de parler: impossible! C'est comme si le lien général de son être se dissolvait; et, ne résistant plus, Antoine tombe sur la natte" (pp. 526–27). In a letter to Louise (Colet (8 July 1853), Flaubert describes his hallucinatory attacks as a kind of hemorrhage of the imagination in which a hundred thousand images leap up like a firework display. The soul seems to leave the body and effects the deathlike loss of consciousness. Again, writing to Mlle Leroyer de Chantepie (18 May 1857), he describes hallucination as the shipwreck of the self. And in the famous exchange with Taine on the difference between creative imagination and hallucination,[16] he describes hallucination as the complete loss of personality, radical *dépaysement,* and terror. All these descriptions perfectly apply to Antoine's explosion of hallucination. Antoine is bled of both interiority and personality by the chaotic shapes which threaten his being. They swarm and multiply, creating their own dizzying temporal urgency. In face of this void, language is ineffectual. The only possible exit is through the loss of consciousness.

    This overwhelming hallucination is a key articulation in the *Tentation de saint Antoine.* It marks the point at which Antoine makes a radical transition into the world of fantasy, but at the same time it again raises the question of creating *enchaînement* between fantasies. If the radical structure of the fantasy is one of separation from the negation of the fantasizing subject, then the possibility of ordering fantasies through the persona of that subject collapses. The fantasy defies both organic growth and temporal unity. Images blink on and off like lights, build up a dizzying momentum, and then fade out.

    After this crisis, the moments of respite between Antoine's fantasies diminish. He wakes from his faint to recognize his familiar straw mat but immediately imagines it is a boat and starts off on a marvellous voyage. With scarcely a transition, he returns to his cabin only to contemplate the metamorphosis of his simple utensils into the luxurious objects of his desire—delicate viands and sumptuous jewels. Again without transition, this scene fades and he finds himself in Alexandria.

    Whereas in the violent explosion of fantasy Antoine lost consciousness, in the Alexandrian sequence his relation to hallucina-

La Tentation de saint Antoine: The Order of Fantasy

tion is that of the dreamer to the dream. The dream substitutes fantasy for reality but maintains a mood in which the dreamer is incorporated. Like that of the dreamer, Antoine's vision knows no temporal limitations. At first he observes the scene from a fixed standpoint: "En face de lui s'étend le lac Maréotis, à droite la mer, à gauche la campagne et immédiatement sous ses yeux, une confusion de toits plats. . ." (p. 528). But, with inhuman range, his eye embraces every aspect of the Alexandrian scene. Like a telescope, it focuses on the most distant objects; like a camera it moves in from the panorama of the two ports to the lighthouse tower, and then to the detail of the burning coals on its summit. It passes from the general perspective to the small and hidden detail, and grasps disconnected fragments with hallucinatory accuracy: the ivory incrustations of the ships in the port, the scraps of meat and fish littering the street, the leprous skin on the shoulder of the priest of Osiris. The impersonal *on* of the narrator embodies Antoine's all-seeing eye: ". . . on aperçoit dans un faubourg des fabriques de verre, de parfums et de papyrus." His complete passivity enables Antoine to glide unhindered from one experience to the next and, finally, to drift out of his own skin into the characters of his fantasy. Thus, he can read the thoughts of Nebuchadnezzar and assume his identity: "Antoine lit, de loin, sur son front, toutes ses pensées. Elles le pénètrent, et il devient Nabuchodonosor" (p. 530). The temporality of this sequence is a continuous presence, absorbing even cataclysmic events, such as the invasion of the Solitaries, in a ritualized present moment: "Les Solitaires sont maintenant dans la ville. Leurs formidables bâtons, garnis de clous, tournent comme des soleils d'acier. On entend le fracas de choses brisées dans les maisons. Il y a des intervalles de silence. Puis de grands cris s'élèvent" (p. 528).

The sudden explosion of images of Antoine's previous hallucination and the dream sequence at Alexandria prefigure the two ways Antoine relates to the world of fantasy: it threatens either to negate him or to incorporate him. In other words, Antoine's dramatic interplay with his fantasies repeats, on another level, the alternation between the temptation to nothingness and the temptation to matter explicit in the content of his hallucinations. From this point of view, his final desire to be matter is at the same time

La Tentation de saint Antoine: The Order of Fantasy

a willingness to be entirely incorporated into fantasy. Both negation and incorporation mean the destruction of the self.

Within the fantasies this loss of self is apparent in the weakness of Antoine's dialogue. In his first encounter with a personified fantasy, the Queen of Sheba, he does not speak at all. He sighs or trembles at her insistent cajolery which he can only overcome by making the sign of the cross. When he does engage in dialogue with his fantasies, his language is not self-illuminating but perpetuates the deceptive world he has created. The more this world grows, the more it consumes the saint and his language. At first he tries to parry Hilarion's theological arguments, but since they are basically the reflection of his own thoughts, he privately defers to them. When Hilarion turns from devil's advocate into the devil himself, he mutely touches his crucifix. In the tremendous babel of the heretics, he hazards the isolated comment or expression of surprise, but the exoticism and profusion of the scene—as in the ritual of the Ophites—force him into passive contemplation. With Apollonius, the procession of the gods, the devil, death, and lust, the visions speak and Antoine listens or else contemplates them in growing fascination. Antoine has no *reasons* with which to dispel them and passes from one to another either by falling unconscious or by the resistance of a gratuitous faith. The tableaux of the gods evoke in him the joyful submission which prefigures his final defeat. Dazzled by the procession of primeval forms, he equates a return to purely material existence with Being. His loss of self reaches its fulfillment in his desire to be matter—which Flaubert explicitly equates with the eclipse of language: ". . . les Bêtes fantastiques—en commençant par les plus éloignés du monde réel—dans la pensée chrétienne la bête semble cacher dessous un esprit. C'est pour cela qu'Antoine voudrait saisir ce qu'il y a en dessous progressivement, elles l'envirent, l'abrutissent, il voudrait entrer dans la nature animale. *La parole arrive à lui manquer.* [*Sic.* My italics.][17]

Although Flaubert's description of the way Antoine enters the world of fantasy and his relation to this world is psychologically convincing, he does not thereby create continuity between the fantasies. On the contrary, since each scene threatens either to negate or incorporate Antoine, it in turn must be radically ne-

La Tentation de saint Antoine: The Order of Fantasy

gated for there to be a possibility of the next scene. The lack of *enchaînement* between scenes is inevitable, given that they can proceed only with the eclipse of their point of origin, the consciousness of Antoine. Significantly, the moments of transition constitute a void or pure gratuitousness marked by Antoine's loss of consciousness or the sign of the cross. The negative moment prefaces an increasing intensity and complexity of fantasy and a diminishment in the self of Antoine. This spiralling structure, however, is not dialectical. Antoine does not pass from one fantasy to another by a negation in which he assimilates previous states of consciousness but by a negation which breaks with the previous states. In fact, the raison d'être of the increasing power and *evil* of Antoine's fantasies resides less in Antoine's own consciousness than in the order of temptations as interpreted in Christian theology. It is an external order. One is reminded of Dante's descent into Hell in which the progressive seriousness of sins is represented by progressively diminishing circles and in which he passes from one circle to the next by loss of consciousness.

Flaubert was obsessed by the structure of the spiral. In fact, the subject of *La Spirale,* the projected novel which exists only in the form of a plan,[18] is a painter who progressively substitutes hallucination for reality and ends up, in the eyes of the world, a madman, but a madman who has discovered the "ensemble of time, the absolute." Many of the painter's hallucinations recapitulate those of Antoine: he imagines a peaceful Pythagorean life with a Brahmin, he understands the language of the animals, he can see plants growing, he grasps the synthesis of past, present, and future, he converses with the gods, and sees the original Types. However, the painter's fantasies develop dialectically with his actions. Good actions give him hallucinatory visions of paradise, and vice versa. Dream has a moralizing influence on life, and life inspires the dream. However, the *Tentation* inverts the meaning of *La Spirale* by making absorption into the world of fantasy a *negative* process. It is identified with a radical evil.

What Flaubert rejects in both the painter's quest for the supreme fantasy and Antoine's desire for the absolute is "the ineptitude which consists in the wish to conclude." In a letter to Louise Colet (8 February 1852) he writes: "La recherche de la cause est

La Tentation de saint Antoine: The Order of Fantasy

antiphilosophique, anti-scientifique, et les religions en cela me déplaisent encore plus que les philosophies, puisqu'elles affirment de la connaître.... Nous serions Dieu, si nous tenions la Cause.... Le matérialisme et le spiritualisme me semblent deux impertinences.... Tous ignorants, tous charlatans, tous idiots qui ne voient jamais qu'un côté de l'ensemble." In this interesting passage, which should have laid to rest the suggestion that Flaubert seeks omniscience through the knowledge of causes (the aesthetics of Jules), he explicitly rejects what he calls the impertinences of idealism and materialism, those dualities which see only one side of the whole. What he affirms is alienation from both cause and conclusion. As we see with Antoine, the quest for the absolute through either pure spirit or matter means the negation or brutalization of his self: the death of language.

Given Flaubert's rejection of the validity of an *enchaînement* dependent upon the idea of causality, it appears paradoxical that he should have attempted to create an aesthetic *enchaînement* in the *Tentation* by relating Antoine's fantasies to a psychological origin. His failure to integrate Antoine's fantasies within a seamless continuum demonstrates that, even on the psychological level, fantasy cannot be reduced to its source and that the relation between the self and hallucination is a negative and discontinuous one.

However, it is not only the discontinuity between Antoine and his fantasies that accounts for the hybrid quality of the *Tentation*. A more radical and aesthetically important discontinuity exists between the form of the dialogue, the dramatic interplay between Antoine and his fantasies, and a third-person narration which, although essential for its advancement, continually interrupts the dialogue form. As previously indicated, Valéry was keenly aware of the hybrid nature of the *Tentation* and attributed it to a struggle between an omniscient scholar pulling his erudite strings and a saint vainly groping for existential cohesion. Certainly, Antoine does not succeed in assimilating his various visions in new syntheses of the self. Given the psychological truth that Antoine is manipulated by his hallucinations into which all the scholarly and theological debates of his time are integrated, it would be beside the point to wish that Antoine should be an organizing center. However, the third-person narrator who moves Antoine from one

La Tentation de saint Antoine: The Order of Fantasy

fantasy to another is not an objective and dissociated scholar. His point of view is very complex and has profound implications for Flaubert's aesthetic development.

Right at the beginning of the *Tentation,* a third-person narrator sets the scene. He is not omniscient, however, but identifies with the limited perspective of an audience focusing upon a stage. His point of view is essentially spatial: he has a right and a left, a background and foreground. As the stage disintegrates into the content of Antoine's visions, the narrator increasingly takes the point of view of the eye of Antoine. It is as though the audience, a generalized *on* which can best be compared to an eye, sees Antoine and at the same time what Antoine sees. Unlike a conventional drama in which the perspective of the audience is silently taken for granted, the *Tentation* incorporates this third person's eye as an essential component in its unfolding. With the eclipse of Antoine's self under the onslaught of fantasy, the third-person narrator increasingly comes into focus. The inessential stage directions of the conventional drama become an essential and explicit part of Antoine's drama.

Nor does Flaubert wish to create the illusion of a transparent third-person narrator, which he could have done by treating Antoine's experience from the point of view of an omniscient third person. He constantly introduces this narrator as a presence, side by side with Antoine. Most often this presence is communicated by the intrusive *on.* In the dream sequence in Alexandria, for instance, one sees what Antoine sees but at the same time the presence of this *on* is explicitly indicated: ". . . on aperçoit dans un faubourg des fabriques de verre, de parfums et de papyrus." Similarly, in the scene of the Ophites, we watch Antoine contemplating the crowd as he waits for the ritual of the snake to begin, and discover our own presence in the point of view of the *on*: sitting along the wall are groups of women, their heads dozing on their knees, so lost in their veils that "on dirait des tas de hardes le long du mur" (p. 541). Similarly, as Antoine watches the Christians awaiting their martyrdom, we are aware of the noise outside of their cells: ". . . *on* dirait le bourdonnement d'une foule et la splendeur d'un jour d'été" (p. 542). Again, in the scene of the Indian gods who multiply and proliferate in a crazy pyramid, Antoine finds it impossible to separate one form from

129

La Tentation de saint Antoine: The Order of Fantasy

another, and *"On* ne distingue pas les prunelles des etoiles, les images des banderoles" (p. 552). Thus, the viewer is conscious of both Antoine's and his own perspective at the same time.

Similarly, the absence of an omniscient point of view is expressed through the tense of this third-person narration, namely, a continually unfolding present reconstructing the presentness of Antoine's visions. Sometimes, as in the first explosion of images which leaves Antoine unconscious, this movement is fragmented, jerky, chaotic; sometimes, as in the scene in Alexandria, it resembles that of a camera, moving in for the close shot and out for the panoramic view; in the scene of the Indian gods, it builds up a fresco-like picture piece by piece; in Antoine's ultimate vision of the primeval monsters, it describes a gradual progression from complex to simple forms, the process of evolution in reverse.

Unlike *La Spirale,* which asserts that hallucination is a privileged modality of being, offering insights into the teleology of nature, the *Tentation,* by means of the restricted point of view of the third-person narrator and the use of the present tense, checks Antoine's desire to reach the absolute—absolute origin or absolute end—through hallucination. By describing the content of a vision, it does not reduce that vision to either a psychological or a historical causality. The vision is other than any hypothetical source. In fact, it becomes an absurdity to attempt to separate Flaubert's perspective from the content of his perspective, just as it is absurd to separate the eye from what the eye sees. The *Tentation* completely reverses the aesthetics of Jules in the *Éducation sentimentale,* which states that art reflects a natural causality and "anticipates" the last word, the teleology implicit in nature. The lack of *enchaînement* in the *Tentation* is the very antithesis of Jules' ideal principle of *enchaînement.* Like Jules, like the Flaubert of *Par les Champs et par les grèves,* Antoine wishes to find the material connection between image and natural fact. By distancing himself from Antoine, by revealing the discrepancy between the image and "reality," a discrepancy Antoine himself does not see, Flaubert in the *Tentation* establishes the basis for a completely new aesthetics.

After the dark night in which he has attempted to coincide with a reality beyond mediating forms, Antoine rediscovers the

La Tentation de saint Antoine: The Order of Fantasy

face, the *figura*, of Christ in the disk of the sun and once again begins to pray. If we are to compare, as seems inevitable, Antoine to Flaubert, it is in their common acceptance of the gratuitous reality of the *figura*. In his acceptance of Christ Antoine sacrifices the inauthentic gratifications demanded by his worldly self and the hubristic desire to penetrate matter and spirit; in his acceptance of the gratuitousness of the image, the figure of speech, Flaubert likewise sacrifices the claims of his own inauthentic personality—still evident in the *Mémoires, Novembre,* and the first *Éducation*—and the desire for a language that would either communicate the infinite or coincide with matter. In the *Tentation* such dualities cease to be meaningful, as does the effort to reduce them to a single principle. Thus Flaubert wrote to Louise Colet (9 May 1852) when he had finished the first version of the *Tentation* and was working on *Madame Bovary*: "Je n'adopte pas quant à moi, toutes ces distinctions de coeur, d'esprit, de forme, de fond, d'âme ou de corps: tout est lié dans l'homme." However, the inherent conflict between Antoine's desire to find the source of forms and a style which reveals such a desire to be an illusion points to a conflict within language itself: in spite of, or rather because of, its gratuitously figural reality, it is tempted to negate itself by positing its origin in some hypothetical material source and its end in some hypothetical transcendence.

NOTES

1. The only work Flaubert wrote between the *Éducation* and the *Tentation* was *Par les Champs et par les grèves,* which he jointly composed, each writing alternate chapters, with Maxime Du Camp. It is a record of a journey they made through Brittany and Touraine; only a fragment was published during Flaubert's lifetime.
2. Throughout this chapter I shall be referring to the text of the last, and definitive, version of the *Tentation*.
3. The MSS of Flaubert's very rough notes to the *Tentation* are in the Bibliothèque Nationale, NAF 23670. For the above reference see fol. 78, recto. Apart from adding accents, I shall make no corrections to these notes.

La Tentation de saint Antoine: The Order of Fantasy

4. Jean Seznec, "Saint Antoine et les monstres," PMLA 58, no. 1 (March 1943), part 1.
5. Alfred Lombard, *Flaubert et saint Antoine* (Paris, 1934), p. 59.
6. NAF 23670, fol. 14, recto.
7. Paul Valéry, "La Tentation de (saint) Flaubert," *Variété 5,* (Paris, 1945).
8. Ibid., p. 203.
9. Victor Brombert, *The Novels of Flaubert* (Princeton, 1966), p. 216.
10. NAF 23670, fol. 64, recto.
11. Ibid., fol. 41, verso.
12. Ibid., fol. 64, recto.
13. Ibid.
14. Ibid.
15. Ibid., fol. 106, recto.
16. See H. Taine, *Vie et correspondance* (Paris, 1902–07), 2: 231–236.
17. NAF 23670, Ibid.
18. Fisher, "Un inédit de Gustave Flaubert."

6

Conclusion

Through its explicit theme and implicit form, the *Tentation* puts into question the dualism that had undermined the *Mémoires, Novembre,* and the *Éducation* of 1845. At the same time, it stands in an interesting and complex relation to *Madame Bovary, Salammbô,* and the *Éducation* of 1868. Flaubert returned to his "vieille toquade," after *Madame Bovary* (and before *Salammbô*) and again after the *Éducation,* as a relief from the special discipline demanded by the "realistic" novel; but in the different phases of its composition, he also incorporated the insights he had acquired while writing his novels. The *Tentation* thus appears to be both an alternative to and an extension of the novel form.

The claim of the realistic novelist, of which Balzac has become the prototype, is that he is writing truth, not fiction. Truth, in this context, means the documentation of life in its socioeconomic and psychological dimensions. The novelist is therefore not an inventor but a witness, an omniscient witness, who can grasp reality in an unmediated way and understand its laws. That Balzac was well aware that this was a grand illusion created by a very adept conjuror does not change the fact that his appeal for the majority of his readers is that when they open his books they have the vivid impression of entering a coherent but particularly exciting and dynamic slice of life. The extraordinary innovation of *Madame Bovary*, however, was that while he created a vivid

Conclusion

realistic picture of provincial Normandy and the torment of an imaginative woman trapped in banality, Flaubert made the reader aware that reality was not an absolute but could be grasped only through very particular and partial perspectives and, more importantly, that coherence was really the property of fiction.

In *Madame Bovary* he maintains a perfect equilibrium between the evocation of a frame of reference outside of fiction and a fictional self-consciousness. The reader is simultaneously aware of the fatality of the materialism governing Madame Bovary's life and of the apparent fatality of the aesthetic form. Many critics have remarked on the airlessness of this novel. Not only does Flaubert create a tight structural symmetry, but his use of objects, which in the first chapters of the novel is realistically descriptive, becomes increasingly symbolic. Like images in a poem, the images of *Madame Bovary* accumulate coherence by an internal system of reference and cross reference. This fine balance of the novel, in which we seem both to be looking transparently out at the world and inwards at the fictional imagination, depends upon a rigid control of complex narrative perspectives.

In *Salammbô* the tension collapses.[1] In spite of the tremendous scholarship and verification of facts with which Flaubert established the infrastructure of the work, reference to the "real" world is strangely insubstantial. And the tight control of imagery which characterizes *Madame Bovary* becomes in *Salammbô* a Parnassian indulgence in the exotic for its own sake. Descriptive passages do not form recognizable scenes but heap detail upon detail until the reader's vision blurs and he retains only a general impression of profusion and exoticism. The lyrical and the real part company, and the result is distortion. The disproportion between a high-flown style and a minutely documented subject matter puts both into serious question.

With the *Éducation sentimentale,* Flaubert's novelistic technique undergoes a profound evolution. Proust was the first critic to grasp the unusualness of its temporal structure.[2] He was aware that the keen sense of the inner temporality of consciousness which Flaubert had created did not correspond to a continuum, a Bergsonian plenum of becoming, but was made up of varied temporal processes, the most startling variation being the interrup-

Conclusion

tion of an inward perception of time—sustained by the use of the imperfect tense—by a sudden "blank." As an example, Proust quotes the famous moment when Frédéric, in stunned amazement, sees Sénécal shoot Dussardier. The shot puts an end to the temporal flow, and the "blank" which follows effects a movement into a time which is no longer measured in minutes but in years and decades.

Flaubert achieves this effect by abolishing a unifying omniscient perspective and grounding his point of view in the consciousness of Frédéric. At the same time, he radically modifies the Balzacian conception of the fictional hero. Frédéric can hardly be called a participant in the whirling life of Paris; he is in the midst of it, but he is for the most part a spectator. Energy and action depend upon discerning an order of meaning, and there are no "laws" to guide Frédéric. Although he attempts to make Mme Arnoux the ordering center of experience, she proves again and again to be a vanishing point, and the course of his private life is primarily directed by mood and impulse. Likewise, he perceives history—into which he is plunged with the revolution of 1848—in its immediate, contingent, and fundamentally chaotic particularity. He cannot interpret events through an abstract point of reference; he perceives them as a series of sensuous, and primarily visual, impressions. The realistic novel, in which objects seem to point to a psychological and social meaning external to themselves, thus yields to a presentation of objects as hallucinatory and unsymbolic images.

Whereas *Madame Bovary* maintains an equilibrium between the evocation of the "real" world and fictional self-consciousness, the *Éducation* makes the real world appear unreal and at the same time creates a work of fiction which undermines the notion of the perfect orderliness and object-like perfection of art. Although he had a pyramid in mind as the structural model of the *Éducation,* Flaubert was aware that the finished novel gives the impression of centerless asymmetry. Whereas the seamlessness of the fictional order of *Madame Bovary*—the constant reprise of previous themes and increasingly symbolic weight of objects—sustains the reader in a quite solid world of the imagination, the sweeping movement of the *Éducation,* the sudden blank spaces, the hallucinatory use

Conclusion

of objects, produces the effect, rather, of the dynamic precariousness and even demonism of the imagination. Seen from this perspective, the movement from the *Éducation* to the *Tentation de saint Antoine* is not an arbitrary one.

With the *Tentation*, Flaubert takes the dissolution of the realistic novel a step further. He does away with society altogether and drains Antoine of every conventional aspect of "character." The desert hermit becomes a vehicle not for sensuous perceptions but for pure fantasies, for images without reference to an immediate and present frame of reference. Thus, the questions Flaubert raises in the *Tentation* become, more explicitly, questions concerning the nature of fantasy and the imagination.

Still, the *explicit* subject matter of the *Tentation* is philosophical and theological rather than poetic, and in this sense there is more content in this work than in Flaubert's novels. However, the explicit content is constantly put into an ironic mode by the implicit form. The result for the reader is that he may well be bored by this undramatic drama and by the decadent genre of the neo-Faustian debates—traces of a lapsed romanticism—if he neglects Flaubert's ironic distance and the innovations of his narrative technique. The *Tentation* makes explicit the implicit themes of Flaubert's major novels, the impossibility of reaching transcendence either through pure subjectivity or pure materiality. It is therefore misleading to speak of the origin and purpose of the imagination, since its being does not reside in a chronological past or future but in a present which has to be continually reconstituted. Its constitutive nature brings into focus both the presence/absence of the subject and the presence/absence of the object. Inseparable from it is a basic ambivalence and precarious temporality. It is in this sense that Baudelaire understood the *Tentation*'s great appeal for "poets and philosophers": it probes the very being of figurative language.

In his study of Flaubert Sartre points out that two completely dissimilar literary movements, naturalism and symbolism, both recognized themselves in Flaubert. The naturalists saw fiction as a reflection of the ensemble of biological, social, and economic factors making up "real"—inevitably sordid—life; the symbolists, on the other hand, valorized the imagination inasmuch as it did

Conclusion

not reflect reality. That they could both claim an affiliation to Flaubert, Sartre suggests, is due to a radical error in Flaubert's aesthetics, that of attributing his negative, derealizing imaginative consciousness to objective reality, thus interpreting the latter as being irrevocably fallen. However, it becomes clear with the *Tentation* that Flaubert refuses to acknowledge either a transcendent imagination or a reality that can be grasped in total objectivity. The imagination dwells in ambivalence. It is because they laid stress either on the material referent of the image or else its insubstantiality qua image that the naturalists and symbolists could both affiliate themselves to Flaubert.

More recently Flaubert has been called a precursor of impressionism, surrealism, and even of the cinema. Indeed, the *Tentation de saint Antoine* brings to a climax an extraordinary concentration on visual effects. In all his work the central metaphor is that of seeing, and he frequently gives his characters an explicit connection to painting. The hero of *Novembre* wished he had been a painter; the hero of the projected *La Spirale* is a painter whose inner visions transcend anything he could paint; and, unsure whether his genius will be that of poet or painter, Frédéric, influenced by the milieu of Madame Arnoux, opts for painting. A painting inspired the *Tentation* and a stained-glass window "Saint Julien l'Hospitalier." *Madame Bovary* existed first as a general tonality—that of gray mold—in Flaubert's mind; and in *Salammbô* he wished to create the general impression of a purple color.

The brothers Goncourt observed that, like a painter, Flaubert had a horror of the blank page and would rapidly cover it with words before beginning the labor of composition. In his letters to Taine on the process of creation,[3] he testified to his keen visual memory: with his eyes closed, he could visualize every detail of a fictional scene. Moreover, he compared his method of composition to the building up of a fresco. Like Antoine's hallucinations, scenes would pass before his eyes which he had to capture before they disappeared into nothingness. He called his relation to reality a "rapport d'oeil" and literature an absolute way of *seeing.* Taine's somewhat unimaginative suggestion to Flaubert was that such a state of mind which constantly visual-

Conclusion

ized physical details, such "vision," could be better transmitted by painting than by writing. Flaubert answered merely that this was not only his state of mind but the modern state of mind, "l'état d'esprit moderne."

It is therefore not surprising that such "modern" manifestations of the primarily visual, such as impressionism, surrealism, and the cinema, should see evidence of their techniques in Flaubert. The trouble with the analogy of the literature of Flaubert to painting, even to impressionism, is that it leaves out its particularity as *literature*. In spite of the sense of insubstantiality created by impressionistic painting, the image, caught in the instant, cannot possibly communicate the complex temporal flow of a literary work. The *Tentation* in particular has been called a precursor of surrealism, and, undeniably, the whirl of uninterpreted images which entrap Antoine testifies to a particularly modern form of consciousness which can no longer constitute a coherent world. At the same time, this perception of phenomena in their randomness turns into intense hallucination, signalling a release of the imaginative consciousness, albeit on a chaotic level. But these aspects of Antoine's fantasies, which one can find both in surrealistic painting and in literature, are specifically named by Flaubert as errors. The world of fantasy which besets Antoine seems to be autonomous, but it is also mechanical and involuntary and bears no constitutive relation either to subjectivity or to a material referent. Dissociated from both, it becomes pure appearance.

The comparison of Flaubert's technique to that of the cinema is particularly tempting and particularly dangerous. As Robbe-Grillet—whose technique has also been called cinematographic—has written, the meaning of description in the novel is quite dissimilar from that in the cinema. The novel takes pages to describe an object which, if projected on the screen, could be perceived in an instant. The details of written description constantly threaten to undermine the integrity of a specific object and the integrity of its context. Something is glimpsed, but instead of growing clearer, "the lines of the drawing accumulate, grow heavier and cancel one another out, shift, so that the image is jeopardized as soon as it is created."[4] An object constructed through words rapidly becomes an absent object, and description,

Conclusion

at least in the modern novel, a conscious process of invention and negation. The novel and the cinema share, however, a sense of unfolding temporality in which images are summoned out of a prior darkness to which they inevitably return.

Robbe-Grillet acknowledges that Flaubert caused the old assumptions of the realistic novel to vacillate and prefigured many of the techniques of the New Novel. However, in spite of the revolution he brought about in narrative point of view, in the temporal structure of the novel, in his emphasis on the *imaginary* nature of literature, Flaubert maintains an ambivalence in his work which, although advocated in theory, is often in practice denied by the New Novelist.

Although he insists on the present/absent, destructive/constructive relation of image to object and the constitutive temporality of his novels, Robbe-Grillet creates a world in which the ambivalence of the imagination tends to collapse into absolutes. The totally subjective narrative point of view—everything is perceived from a restricted angle of vision—nevertheless seems to claim a total objectivity. By "objectivity" his critics mean an analytical coldness, but his choice of spatial, mathematical, and, in particular, geometrical imagery to describe objects is specifically aimed at denying the illusion of the "romantic heart" and anthropomorphism of things. Intending to describe merely the "thereness" of objects, his imagery tends towards the nonfigural sign, a formula suggesting the essential law behind but not the existential reality of objects. In this sense, he does not constitute the ambivalent presence/absence of objects but a world of essences and signs. Thus, although the reader is called upon to participate in the temporal constitution of the novel, he finds himself relating to it as to a reified enigma which titillates his ingenuity and concentration but does not wholly engage him. Although in this way Robbe-Grillet sucessfully destroys the illusion of the novel being life, he risks turning it into a word game. The constitutive reality of fiction then lapses into the reified language of signs.

In fact, Robbe-Grillet suggests that the tendency in the novel to break down the old rationalist antinomies might soon find verification in science: "Today's life, today's science are dissolv-

Conclusion

ing many of the categorical antinomies established by the rationalism of the past centuries. It is true that the novel, which like every art, claims to precede systems of thought and not to follow them, should already be in the process of melting down the terms of other pairs of contraries: matter-form, objectivity-subjectivity, signification-absurdity, construction-destruction, memory-presence, imagination-reality, etc."[5] Even if we grant that science might overcome the mechanical dualism on which it was originally based through the discovery of the unity of supposed opposites, unless it acknowledged the constitutive reality of the imagination, it would still, from Flaubert's perspective in the *Tentation*, be in error. Thus, Flaubert goes further than even the foremost exponent of the new novel in refusing to anchor the being of literature in some other sphere. This does not mean a "turning away" from life but a reconstitution of meaning in its full dialectical ambivalence.

NOTES

1. See Nathalie Sarraute, "Flaubert's Style," *Partisan Review*, spring 1966, pp. 57-74.
2. Marcel Proust, "A Propos du style de Flaubert," *Chroniques*, 1920, p. 205.
3. Collected and commented on by Taine in his *Vie et correspondance*.
4. Alain Robbe-Grillet, *For a New Novel*, trans. Richard Howard (New York, 1965).
5. Ibid., pp. 166–67.

Index of Names

Balzac, 11, 28, 133
Baudelaire, 15, 16, 28, 54, 60, 74n., 136
Bonwit, Marianne, 103n
Bouilhet, Louis, 13, 16, 106
Breughel, 105
Brombert, Victor, 16, 119, 132n
Bruneau, Jean, 4, 6, 48, 56, 74n., 85, 96, 98
Byron, 105

Chateaubriand, 18, 48
Chéruel, Adolphe, 18
Coleman, Algernon, 5
Colet, Louise, 3, 5, 7, 8, 12, 13, 43, 69, 76, 101, 102, 124, 127, 131
Collier, Gertrude, 46n
Constant, 32

Dante, 127
Delille, 93
de Man, Paul, 15
Demorest, D.-L., 6, 85
Descharmes, René, 46n
Du Camp, Maxime, 13, 16, 69, 106, 120, 131n
Dumas, 18

Fischer, E. W., 46n., 132n
Flaubert, passim
Freud, 25

Girard, René, 75n
Goethe, 105
Goncourt, brothers, 69, 117, 137

Hugo, 18

Jensen, Wilhelm, 25

Lacan, Jacques, 21

Lamartine, 33
Legrain, *père*, 105
Le Poittevin, Alfred, 120
Leroyer de Chantepie, 124
Lévi-Strauss, Claude, 14
Lombard, Alfred, 116, 117, 118, 132n

Mallarmé, 22
Mérimée, 18
Michelet, 18
Molière, 92
Montaigne, 19, 90
Musset, 19

Pascal, 22, 23
Pouchet, 114
Poulet, Georges, 96, 97, 98, 99, 100 103
Proust, 134, 135, 140n

Quinet, 105

Reik, Theodor, 46n
Renan, 108
Richard, Jean-Pierre, 96, 99, 103, 104n
Robbe-Grillet, Alain, 138, 139, 140n
Rousseau, 19, 23, 33, 48, 75n

Sand, George, 118
Sarraute, Nathalie, 140n
Sartre, J.-P., 6, 7, 8, 13, 30, 41, 42, 43, 46n., 68, 69, 75n., 86, 96, 98, 136
Schlésinger, Elisa, 8, 32, 65
Seznec, Jean, 116, 118, 132n

Taine, 42, 46n., 124, 132n., 137, 140n

Valéry, Paul, 16, 118, 119, 128, 132n
Voltaire, 92

141